Abandoned Places: Abandoned Memories (Desert Edition)

Cover Art

The cover of this book was designed by co-author and book photographer, Julie Ferguson (http://juliefergusondesigns.blogspot.com)

Dedication

We would like to thank the readers of our blogs. They have been eager to follow our road trips and hear of our crazy treks through the desert, as well as encouraging us to put this together in one place for everyone to enjoy. Julie would like to thank her husband, Gary Ferguson, for putting up with our road trips and believing in our project. Sharon would like to thank her son, Alex Clauss, for believing his mom is living up to her potential.

About the Authors

Sharon Day

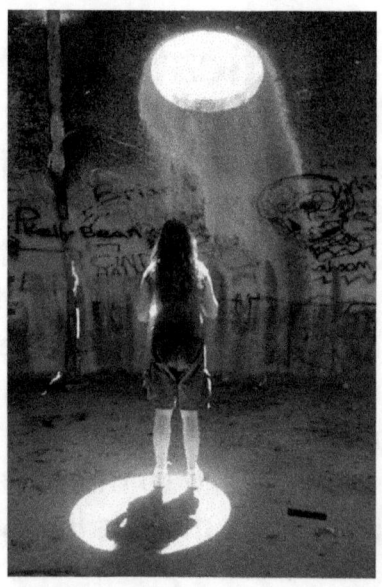

Sharon is a paranormal investigator, psychic, blogger, and author.

Blogs:
www.ghosthuntingtheories.com
www.zombiehousewivesoftheapocalypse.com

Abandoned Places: Abandoned Memories (Desert Edition)

CafePress Shops:
www.cafepress.com/ghosthuntingtheories
www.cafepress.com/zombiehousewivesoft
heapocalypse

Books:
Zombie Housewives of the Apocalypse
Was That a Ghost?
Kickin' Up Dust! Getting Lost To Find
Ourselves
Josiah: Undead Cowboy
Don't Go There! A Flash Horror Anthology
Blogging Changed My Life!

Horror Erotica Line on Kindle as penname
Anna Melissa

Coming Soon Books:
Zombie Housewives of the 1960s
Growing Up With Ghosts
Moon Madness (They Only Come Out At
Night)

Abandoned Places: Abandoned Memories (Desert Edition)

Julie Ferguson

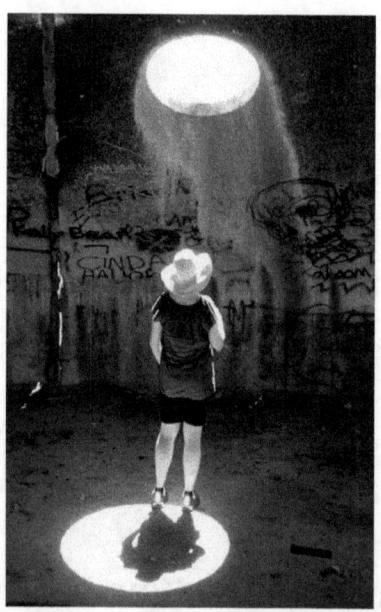

Julie is a paranormal investigator, blogger, author, photographer and graphic artist.

Blogs:
http://above-the-norm.blogspot.com
www.zombiehousewivesoftheapocalypse.com
http://juliefergusondesigns.blogspot.com

Abandoned Places: Abandoned Memories (Desert Edition)

CafePress Shops:
www.cafepress.com/zombiehousewivesoft
heapocalypse.com
www.cafepress.com/backroadstreasures

Etsy Shop:
www.etsy.com/shop/adsila99

Books:
Zombie Housewives of the Apocalypse
Kickin' Up Dust! Getting Lost To Find
Ourselves

Coming Soon Books:
Dead and Buried in the Southwest Desert
Zombie Housewives of the 1960s
Moon Madness (They Only Come Out At
Night)

Abandoned Places: Abandoned Memories (Desert Edition)

Table of Contents

Abandoned Places: Abandoned Memories (Desert Edition)

Introduction

Julie and I met through blogging about paranormal subjects. We went on a ghost hunt, and then on a road trip. Pretty soon, we were hitting the road, photographing and ghost hunting.

It seemed a natural progression for Julie and I to go around the desert and photograph abandoned sites. We both loved the chance to travel the back roads and were fascinated with the shells of buildings left behind in places that were once boom-towns now gone bust.

What makes this book series so intriguing is that we utilized our love for abandoned sites with my skills in psychometry and her skills in photography.

The most basic explanation for psychometry is, "*the ability to touch an object or person and read emotions and memories left behind by the humans who have encountered it.*"

It is a skill I began as a young child digging up Civil War relics at the manor home where I grew up (*a prior field hospital during The War*). I thought everyone had the sense that included touching something and knowing about past handlers of the object. I was in my 20s before I realized most others do not have this ability. It was like finding out that no one sees color and trying to then explain what colors are and how they come together to make the scenes we see.

When we pass by abandoned sites, it is human nature to wonder what it looked like in its heyday or to think about those who had lived there. This book, <u>Abandoned Places: Abandoned Memories (Desert Edition)</u> helps the reader to enjoy not only the way that nature reclaims a building, but to know the life that once resided there still remains in stasis.

These readings are not about actual ghosts haunting the sites, but are of the living that passed by and interacted with the environment and left a memory record to be read by a skilled psychometrist and sometimes by a visitor who gets a sudden chill or feels sad, but doesn't know why.

Some of these stories occurred in the locations in their heyday, others when the locations were in tatters and some did not occur in these locations as the object might have been relocated from its original site.

I learn more about human nature and

people's thought processes, experiences and emotions every time I read an object. Being able to share these finds in story form was a gratifying challenge. Most psychic reads involve another person sitting with me while I tell them their own story. In this case, the stories are lost to time and space. Being able to bring them to life again in the setting of such quiet desolation was very gratifying.

These may all be desert locales, but the characters that have come and gone in these locations are as varied as any city in America. You may even see a bit of yourself in them.

Sharon Day

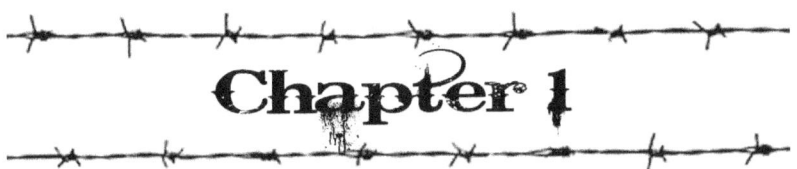

Chapter 1

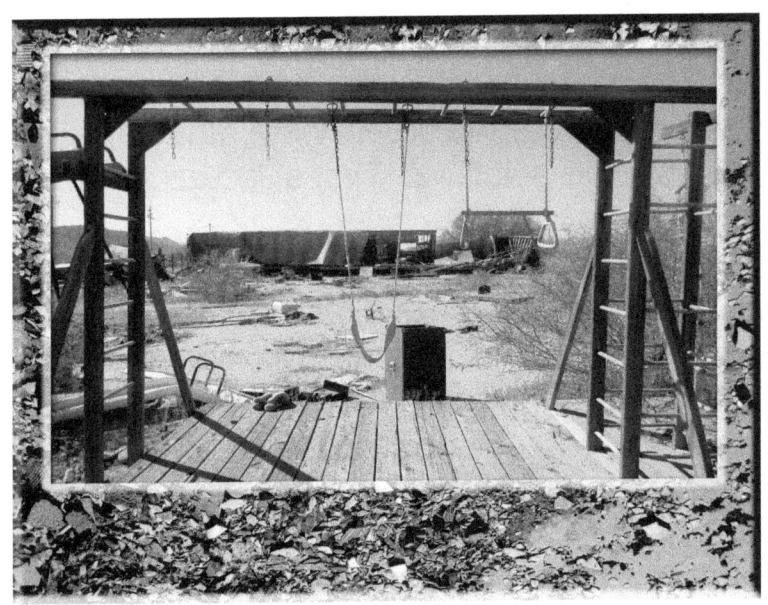

"Little Girl Gypsy"

Abandoned Places: Abandoned Memories (Desert Edition)

Our first stop on the abandoned trek was a place Sharon had been to a few times. The site was chaotic and confusing. It appeared as if some cosmic player had tossed the pieces onto the desert floor with no rhyme or reason. It was either a giant dump for locals or something that began as a trailer park site, but later became a makeshift landfill.

The contents within the trailers and those strewn out across the desert were random; books, photos, suitcases, TVs, a Jacuzzi, a bathtub, toys....

It almost seemed like a thief's dump site, but a careful thief wouldn't take so many things he didn't want to keep. As we walked around under the piercing sunlight, wind howling through the sage and creosote bushes, we tossed out possibilities.

"Maybe someone had the land and let their friends put their trailers here." Julie contemplated as she spun around and studied the debris and collapsing mobile homes. "Maybe the well water ran dry."

Sharon nodded. It was possible. "The big trailer is packed with furnishings, books, and all kinds of odds and ends. Someone was storing things in it. Maybe they used this place as a giant dumping ground for their hoarding stuff."

Julie held onto her wide-brimmed hat and nodded. We wandered, staring down at the items on the ground to keep from stepping on boards with nails, shovels, broken glass, but occasionally lifting our heads to watch a nearby train roar by or a solo huge bird cawing above us.

With so many objects to choose from, determining which one to read was commanded by instincts Sharon used in antique shops to choose an item; *strolling without touching.*

As she wandered in and out of the personal items, the electronics and tools, boards and tiles, clothing and books, she let her body tell her when to stop. She lifted her head to see right in front of her was a swing set. Even though toys lay all around it in a jumbled mess, Sharon knew she wanted to touch the seat of the swing and find out why she was compelled to stop there and stare at it.

When touching an object, the very first thing a psychic notes is good or bad energy; positive or negative feelings; neutrality or even old faded energy that is fuzzy and vague. Next, emotions come forward and male or female energy. Soon, pictures and associations, storylines and connections become clear. It's an odd progression that differs from psychic to psychic. It's a bit like when someone says, "do you recall your prom night?" and it comes to you in pieces that makes out a jumpy scene, but contains emotions, relationships, spatial elements, and senses.

Touching the swing's seat produced a flash of an image in her head. Sharon rarely gets visuals first, but the first thing that came to mind was a knobby kneed, slender little girl with dishwater blond hair and a lip worn with little bruises and dry cracked skin from constant nibbling at it.

Wind howled through the endless open desert and spun granules of sand around her as she looked off into the distance. A train chugged by not a thousand feet from the site, but Sharon didn't even register it rumbling the ground. Her senses were focused on a combination of anxiety and a sadly detached emotional content. As a mother, it tugged at her heart, as a psychic it intrigued her.

Deciding this would be her read for the

Abandoned Places: Abandoned Memories (Desert Edition)

location; Sharon pulled up a scene from this girl's past and focused on it to get to know this "gypsy girl" on an emotional and mental level. Although her sense was that the girl turned out all right in the end, there was a time in the youth's life that was very disturbing and melancholy. The swing set was not likely in this location at the time of this moment in the girl's life, but its residual was still there.

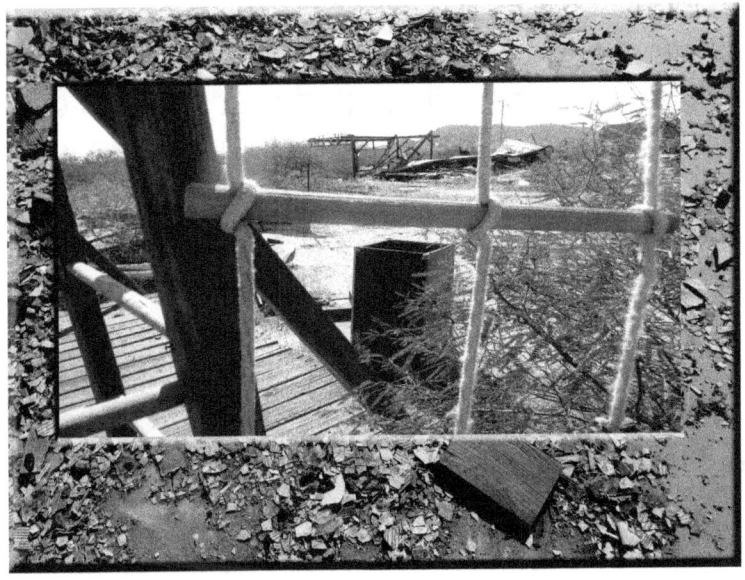

Abandoned Places: Abandoned Memories (Desert Edition)

Abandoned Swing Set

The swing set was not hers. Nothing was hers. She stole toys from other children, coveting them and then, for no reason at all, discarding them without a second thought.

The little girl lived for the moment. She knew she couldn't take anything with her that didn't fit into her mother's suitcase. She tolerated the kids who used the swing set with her only because she didn't realize she could say "no."

Early on, the girl learned that she was on her mother's life ride, a wild one that landed them in new places and with new people constantly. Nothing stayed the same, faces changed, possessions were fleeting. The only thing she counted on was her mother. She liked to keep the distracted woman within her sight or her belly would clench in fear. With everything constantly shifting in her world, the girl feared the importance of her mother being the only permanent feature. It made the flighty woman too precious a commodity to lose.

The girl pumped her legs on the swing for hours on end with nothing in her mind. She didn't dream. She didn't imagine the future. She only lived in the moment. Sometimes, just the sound of the swing set shifting and her breathing as she worked harder and harder to go higher and higher were the only things she focused on. She had no imaginary world to escape to. The only release for her was in the moments when she gave up fighting sleep and fell into slumber.

Two siblings crossed her path in a rush to do some secret task. They whispered and giggled and seemed quite happy with the interactions. The girl stilled on the swing and watched the comfortable camaraderie. The concept of having another child to play with and share things with was foreign to her. As an only child and always on the move, her whole world depended on reading adults' expressions, knowing their intentions and anticipating their moves.

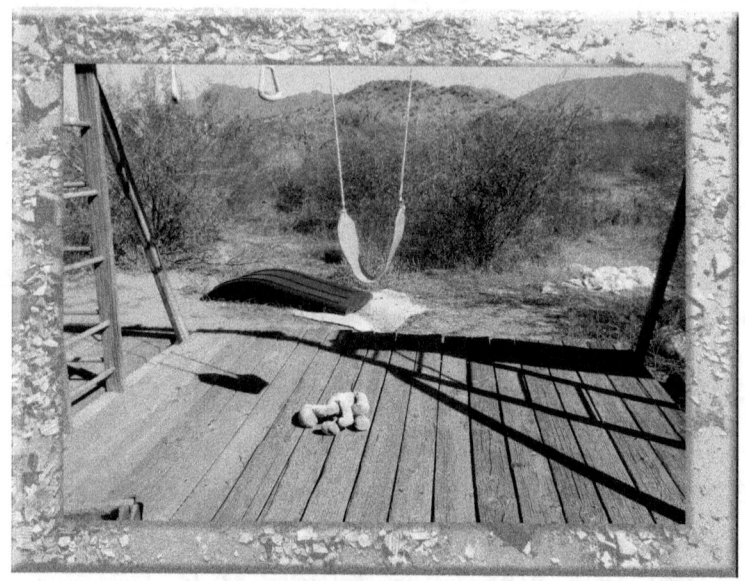

   Often the girl wondered what children had
to talk about. She rarely felt the need to speak.
Perhaps it was because there was no one to talk
to. Her mother only responded to repeated,
"*Mommy? Mommy? Mommy?*" The woman's
reaction was usually a sigh and a tilt of the head.
Then, the girl would become tongue-tied. She
had no real request in mind, just wanted to know
her mom would respond if she called. She tested
her mother's maternal reflex often in moments of
insecurity. After all, if the woman could leave
her new friends so easily, what was to keep her
from leaving the little girl behind with strangers?

Abandoned Places: Abandoned Memories (Desert Edition)

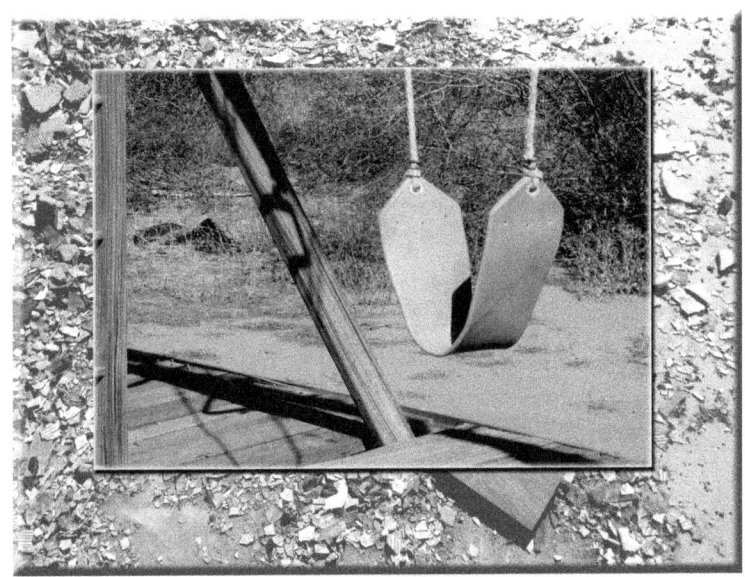

Today, her mother looked very preoccupied as she rushed in and out of the door. The woman lit a cigarette several times in the past hour and the girl knew that meant she was anxious. When her mother was anxious, it meant change was coming. The girl stilled on the swing and held her breath as her mother stomped out another cigarette and went inside. At some point, arguing would begin and their bag would be packed yet again.

It didn't matter to the girl. She was used to the routine and never became comfortable in any one place. None of them were a home, but some of them were more comfortable than others. This one was noisy and dirty and boring. The man didn't bother her, but he also didn't like to talk much. Sometimes, he'd give her the last piece of bacon at breakfast or bring her home a pack of gum. For a moment, she felt like he could see her, like she existed.

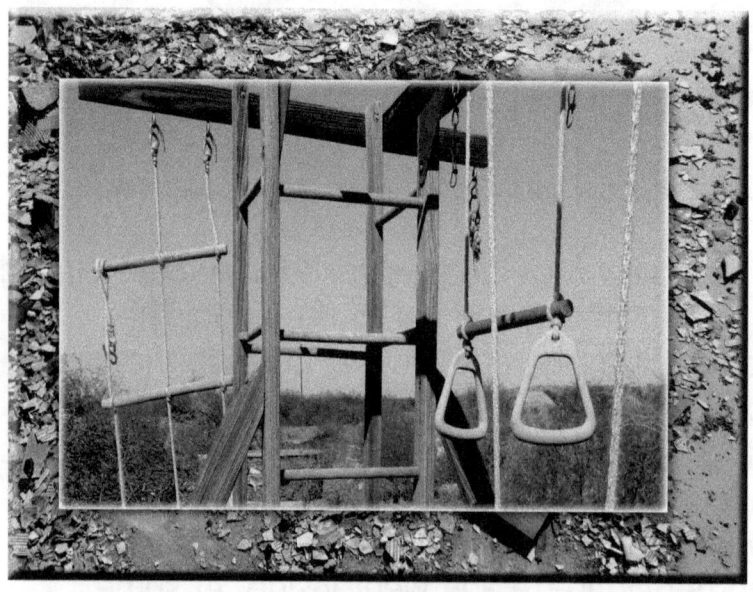

The girl swallowed hard, trying not to think of the trembling feeling in her belly every time she wished to be seen, to be heard, to be acknowledged. She closed her eyes and took a

Abandoned Places: Abandoned Memories (Desert Edition)

deep breath. Her world had no God, but she sometimes pictured things how she might wish them to be.

She wished they could stay. It was hot and dusty and the man grumbled when he watched the news on TV, but he seemed to not mind having a child around and that was better than most of the men they'd stayed with who never so much as acknowledged her.

A little girl with a Raggedy Ann doll stood on the edge of the swing set and watched the lonely child as she pumped harder and harder on the swing, huffing away as she tried to see how high she could go.

She ignored the intruder, but the girl with the doll looked up at her.

"Whatcher name?"

The swinging girl didn't answer. She pretended not to hear her. Perhaps the other girl would go away. Her world had always been around adults and children confused her. She didn't like talking to them or hearing them cry when they fell down or wanting to play silly games. She quit pumping her legs and the swing slowed down. The girl with the doll turned away and then pivoted, turning back to her.

"I'm Emily." The stranger offered.

The gypsy girl dragged her feet on the ground to bring the swing to a stop. Usually if she just stared and said nothing, the other children would leave her alone. This girl, however, came up closer.

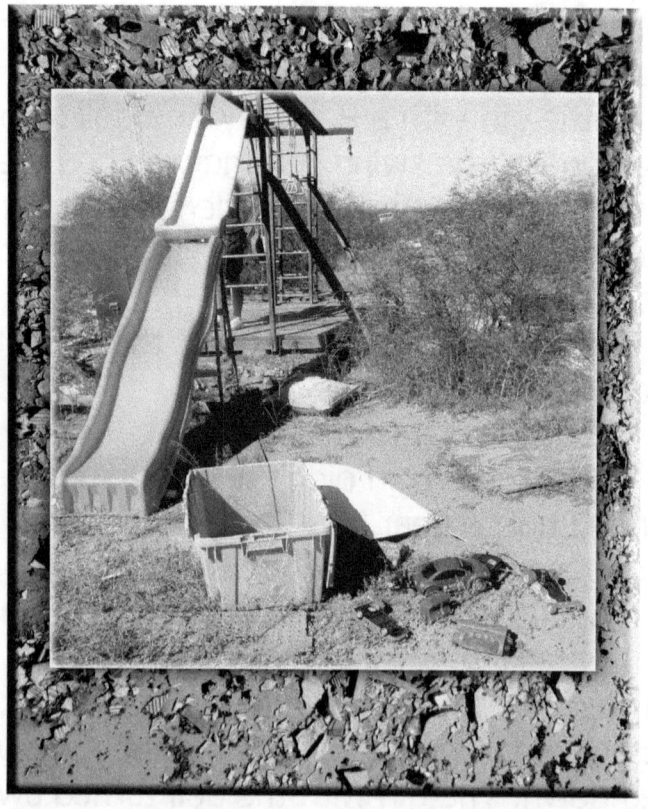

"I'm going to use the slide, okay?"

Abandoned Places: Abandoned Memories (Desert Edition)

She started up the rungs nearby and lifted up her doll, letting it go down the slide first.

The lonely girl saw the doll at the bottom of the slide, face down on the ground. Suddenly, she wanted it more than anything in the world. Her fingers curled around the ropes of the swing and she watched as the other girl prepared to slide down.

Like her impulsive mother, she grabbed it up, tucked it in close to her body and ran towards the door. She turned back before entering and waited for the inevitable wails of the little girl whose toy was taken, but instead it was silent. The "Emily" girl climbed the slide again, having forgotten the doll and went down belly first with a giggle of delight.

The gypsy girl looked at the stolen doll and realized it meant nothing to the other child. She tossed it onto the ground and then stomped on its legs, turning and going inside and out of the harsh sunlight to yet another form of silence and loneliness.

At least, this one was familiar and asked nothing new of her, like talking and playing when she didn't know what to talk about and how to play.

Abandoned Places: Abandoned Memories (Desert Edition)

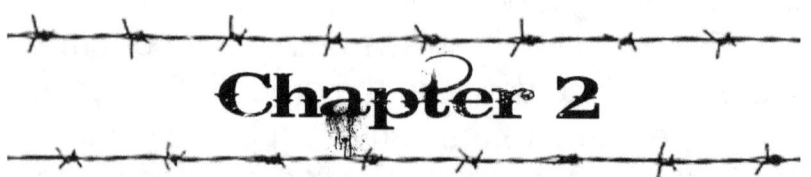

Chapter 2

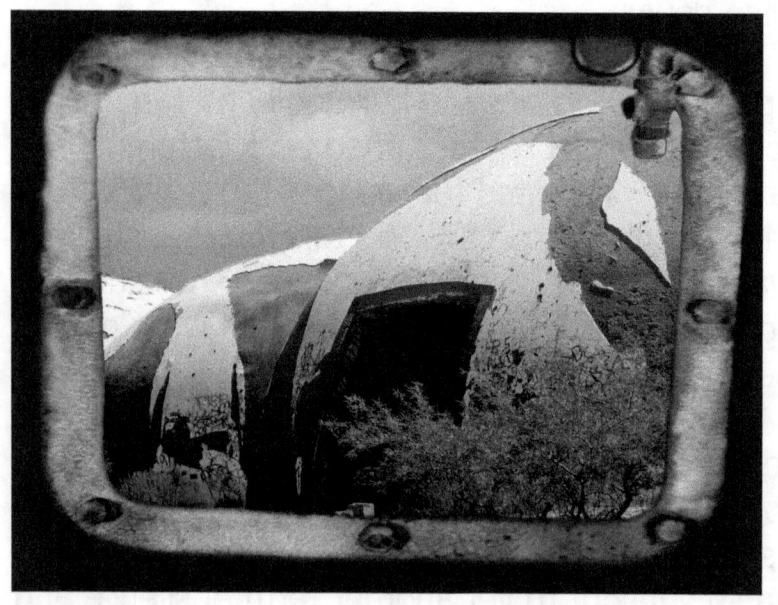

"Outcast Injured Teen"

Abandoned Places: Abandoned Memories (Desert Edition)

This isolated location in a small town in the desert had a bad reputation as the only place for bored teens and indigents to settle in for the night or party.

It was built with the most optimistic hopes to have a unique factory in the Southwest, but the company went under and the site was left abandoned in the relentless sunlight.

Sharon had been there before and was chased out by squatters. This time, we got to investigate uninterrupted to take beautiful pictures and get a read.

The buildings sat in a strange little formation that made no rhyme or reason. They were open and windowless except for cracks in the ceilings letting light in. Their very dome-like shape created ricocheting sounds so loud and tinny that even the softest whisper sounded like a shout. The effect was disturbing in these hanger-like buildings and created a strange fun-house feel, startling us with every footstep.

Getting a psychic read on people altered by drugs and alcohol, emotions and hormones all in one mix is like trying to find the curved pin in a pile of straight pins. There are just too many similar things happening in one space at one

Abandoned Places: Abandoned Memories (Desert Edition)

time and all of them amplified by mind-altering factors and overlapping in nonsensical layers.

Focusing on one individual in this grouping of buildings was very hard. There were no lingering possessions, only castaway tin cans and bottles, lots of graffiti and crumbling bits of plaster.

Sharon tried touching the walls, but the cacophony of past wild teen parties left a blurry maze in her mind. She stopped and stood there a moment, taking it in and then leaned down and touched the floor, a scene unfolding in her mind like a hazy drug-induced memory. It occurred not that far off in the past and while the buildings were the crumbling mess they were the day of the read.

Sometimes, she would get images, other times, a sense of being in someone's point of view without knowing who that person was. In this case, she had a vague sense of a tall slender youth, perhaps 14 or 15 years old with his hair a bit grown out, his clothes purposefully sloppy and his posture slump-shouldered. He seemed to personify a typical adolescent, even down to his vague sense of self. The reason she focused on this youth over any other was because of the physical injury he incurred. It was that shocking moment in time that made her able to hone in on him in a sea of other youths.

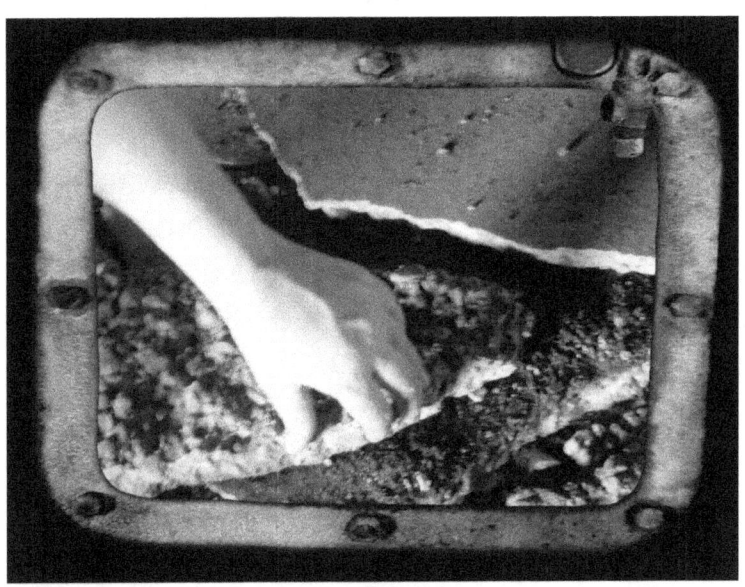

Abandoned Factory

The party started even before darkness came. It was risky having it begin while there was still some light, but no one came down that dusty road and the nearest house didn't look out over the grouping of abandoned hanger-shaped buildings.

Abandoned Places: Abandoned Memories (Desert Edition)

The young teen arrived with his older friends. He was a freshman, but he was tall and wiry. People assumed he was older, although he was still as awkward in his body as any adolescent.

He had no real direction or plan for his life. He was neither smart like his sister nor athletic like his brother. His place in his family was as ill-defined as his place within this group of new friends. He watched silently, as he did at home, waiting for a sign of what he should do, hoping someone would instruct him.

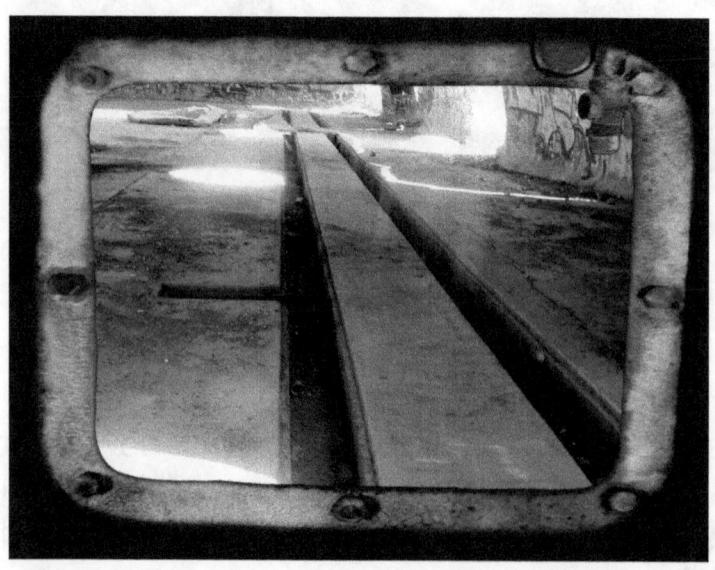

Abandoned Places: Abandoned Memories (Desert Edition)

His new buddy handed him a paper cup with clear liquid in it. He sniffed. *No odor.* He gulped it down like the others and his throat constricted against the burn of vodka. The voices around him sounded as if they were shouting from some distance and his ears rang.

The youth leaned back against the wall to find its shell shape didn't accommodate leaning. He squatted down near where kids had started a fire inside the structure. Gray smoke billowed and the heat staved off the desert chill outside.

One of the older guys in his 20s handed him a beer from a six-pack dangling from his fingers and smiled too enthusiastically to be genuine. The teen stood up and opened the beer.

"Ty tells me you're from Phoenix."

"I was." The youth responded and then drank down the beer, enjoying the fluid feeling creeping into his legs.

"You have any connections?"

When the teen just stared back in confusion, the young man snorted and nodded to Ty. "Your friend's not a stoner, huh?"

"No." Ty told him.

"Damn!" the guy shook his head and

looked like he wanted to take back his beer. "I need a Phoenix connection." He muttered as he wandered off into the dark recesses of the building.

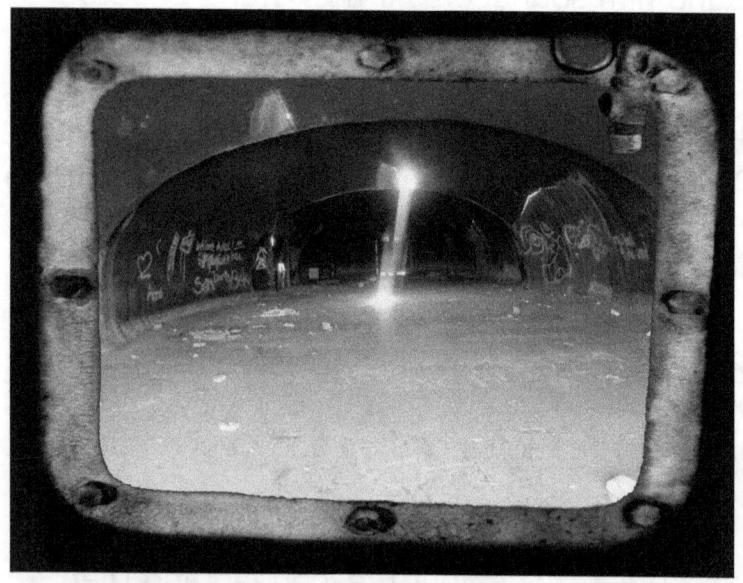

Someone near the fire tossed in a bottle of liquor and it exploded in a whoosh, one of the guys stumbled back into the youth and he fell back against the wall, beer spraying all over him.

Laughter erupted and for a dazed moment, the teen thought everyone was laughing at him. The smoke burned his eyes and he turned away. Ty handed him another drink. He held the vodka in one hand and the beer in the other.

"Just pour in it." Ty nodded.

The youth poured the vodka with a shaking hand into the beer bottle and then drank.

"All at once!" Ty encouraged.

The teen did as he was instructed, feeling a warm numbness spread through his chest and limbs.

He laughed when he lowered the bottle and caught one of the girls looking at him. He smiled at her in a way he never would have braved when sober.

Somebody screamed, followed by laughter as a guy picked up his girlfriend and swung her around. The campfire smoke permeated every breath as the youth downed another cup of vodka. Someone passed him a wine bottle and he took a long swig from it and passed it on.

People came and went, talking to him and smoking until his eyes watered from the fumes of cigarettes, bonfire and pot. He stumbled to the gaping opening of the building and stared out into the black night. He opened up his trousers and took a piss, not thinking to care that he was still in the light of the building. A couple guys passed by him and chuckled and he smiled stupidly as he swayed and tugged at his zipper.

He stood inside the structure and looked around for Ty or Ty's little tag-a-longs, but they were nowhere. The teen worked his way through a group of seniors to the back of the building and then stopped when he entered a cloud of pot smoke. His stomach roiled and he turned away to leave when Ty yelled out.

"No thanks." He waved his hand and stumbled back on unsteady feet. For some reason, his legs wouldn't work right as he made his way back to the burning fire on the floor of the structure.

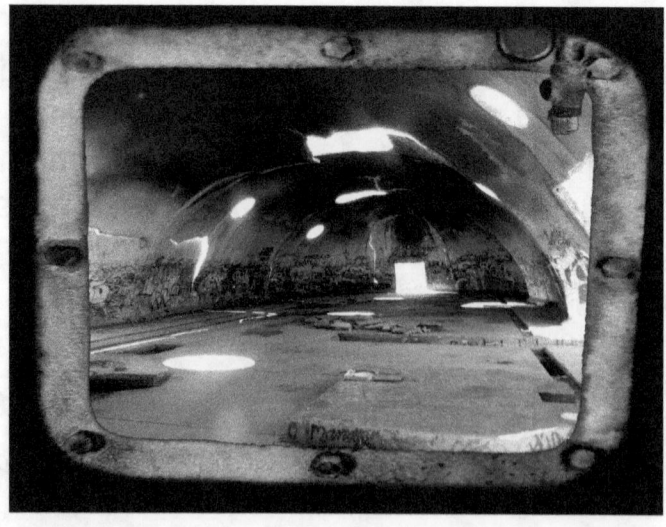

Abandoned Places: Abandoned Memories (Desert Edition)

A girl brushed past him, her breast grazing his arm and the teen felt a giddy thrill as he watched her stride outdoors. Without his usual inhibitions, he followed her, squinting against the light from inside compared to the black desert outdoors.

The sound of giggles made him stop short and teeter on his toes. His stomach began to curdle and he put a fist to his diaphragm, certain he would hurl in any second. The lights of cigarettes in a tight circle showed the group of girls as they chattered and talked.

Abandoned Places: Abandoned Memories (Desert Edition)

The teen turned back indoors and tucked in between the warm fire pit and the wall. The guys were laughing and chucking another bottle onto the fire. It exploded with such gusto, the crumbling walls shook. A large football player backed up into the youth and he fell forward without any instinct to stop himself, hitting the concrete floor face first.

His world came to a fast halt and his arms still wouldn't work. His face was wet and someone was howling nearby. Hands grabbed at him and a few people hoisted him up onto rubbery legs. His face was wet now. Damn! His eyes rolled closed and someone jostled him.

"Dude! You're totally missing your front teeth!" Ty sounded like he was speaking down a long metal tube.

The youth bobbed. A couple guys guided him into the cold air outside and his wet face stung a bit. In fact, he knew he should be hurting after hitting the wall. *Or was it the floor?*

His eyes rolled closed again as they hoisted him into the car and headed into town. He vomited on the floor the car and someone made him lie down where he went into a nice welcome sleep.

Abandoned Places: Abandoned Memories (Desert Edition)

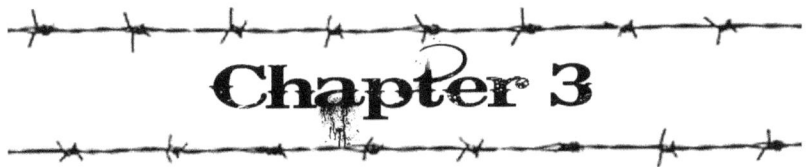

Chapter 3

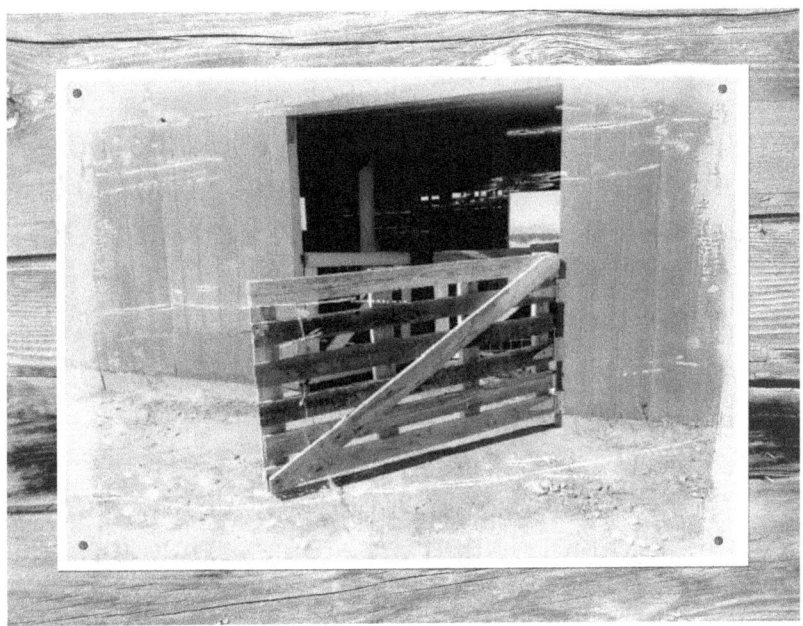

"Man of the Family"

Abandoned Places: Abandoned Memories (Desert Edition)

This was a strange serendipitous find and an amazing realization for Sharon about her psychic talents.

We came across a burned out home for sale and stopped and studied it. Sharon wanted to know what might have happened there, so she went inside and started to touch the charred remains. She moved around from room to room, trying to find something to hone in on, but her mind was completely blank. Becoming irritated with the lack of reads, she poked and prodded and tested every beam, every surface, only to be faced with a startling realization: *She could not get a read on the entire place!*

What did this mean about her abilities? Was she reading something in the surface? Did burning it away rid it of the information or did it change the texture somehow making it to porous to read? Intrigued, she wandered out back to clear her thoughts when the stables came into view.

Untouched by the fire, they promised a potential read, so she entered. More than any of the other reads, she felt herself inside this man of the family's head quite clearly. She stood at the doorway to look out and saw the desert

Abandoned Places: Abandoned Memories (Desert Edition)

through his eyes, his thoughts, his emotions.

He was such a very simple man, it almost made it hard to read him. There were no layers. He simply was what he was and had no access to any depth of conflicting emotions most people struggle with.

Sharon had no idea how long she stood there staring out, but when she turned away, she had all the content she needed to tell this man's story...

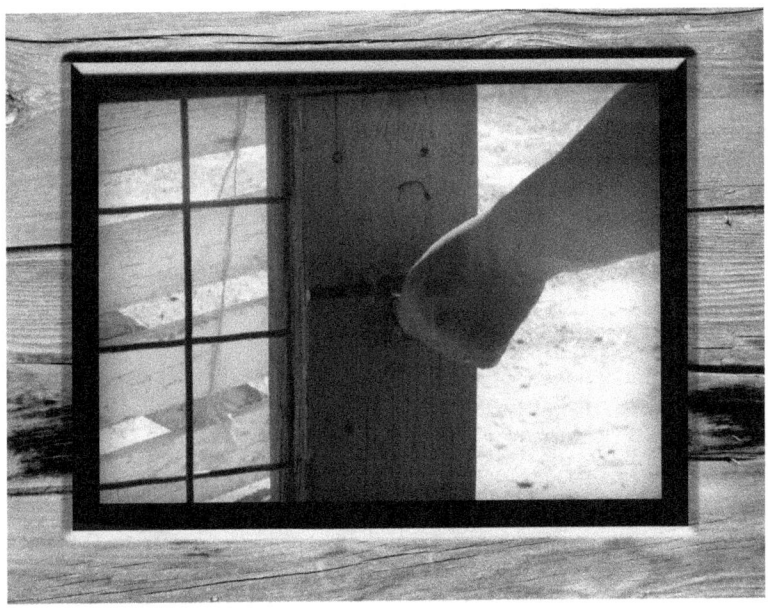

Abandoned Places: Abandoned Memories (Desert Edition)

Abandoned Stables

He straightened out and heard the vertebrae in his back pop and crunch. His muscles felt particularly sore. Perhaps it was the cold morning. It was warming up quickly. He studied the stable's interior and shook his head. There was so much to get done before they hit the road to visit his wife's family. He needed to clean the stalls and exercise the horses. They'd be gone just one night. It wasn't that much of a drive, but he hated any time they had to leave home.

He wiped his hands on his jeans and took a deep breath of the smell of sweet hay and manure, as familiar as the medicinal scent of creosote oils in the desert rain. If he had his way, he'd never leave their land. As far as the eye could see it was open flat desert and scrub brush, sky that never ended and distant craggy purple mountains. All of it, the most beautiful damned sight in the world!

Stiffly he made his way into the dark damp stables. The horses shifted in anticipation of the routine, their tails swooshing, snorting softly. He reached out and put a calming hand on the

Abandoned Places: Abandoned Memories (Desert Edition)

mare's velvety soft nose.

"It's okay." He said softly, speaking more to himself than the horse.

He hated leaving home. It was a childish obsession, but he'd worked hard for a home and a family and it represented something much more than just property.

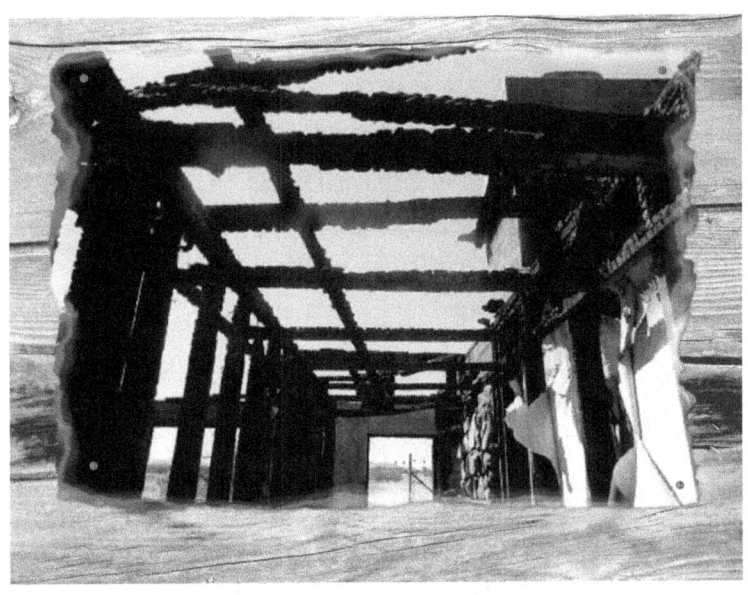

His father was out of the scene when he was still young, but the responsible youth took over the position of man of the family and took that place seriously. His mother depended upon him and his younger siblings looked up to him as someone balanced and predictable, rigid and in control of all the responsibilities. There was comfort in order and routine. Even into middle age, his days were spent in the same pattern. There was no time for hobbies or distractions or entertainment. The very notion of it made his palms sweat.

He absent-mindedly rubbed his hands on his jeans again.

The breeze outside made the gate swing and scream like a cow caught in barbed wire. He went over to secure it and looked out at a dust devil dancing in the distance. Every day he looked at his surroundings as if they were a loved one he may never see again.

He often times said a silent prayer to God for His blessings. The man never wished for more, he only wished to keep what he had. He appreciated it more than most because he needed to be self-made, self-reliant. His property held no surprises, no unknowns. It was as predictable as he. It had no moods, no expectations other than the obvious daily upkeep. He knew his place in the order of things and it was to maintain.

Now, in charge of his own livelihood, he

thrived. His days were long and exhausting, his nights filled with chores the hot desert sun made too tough to accomplish.

This was his heart and his country.

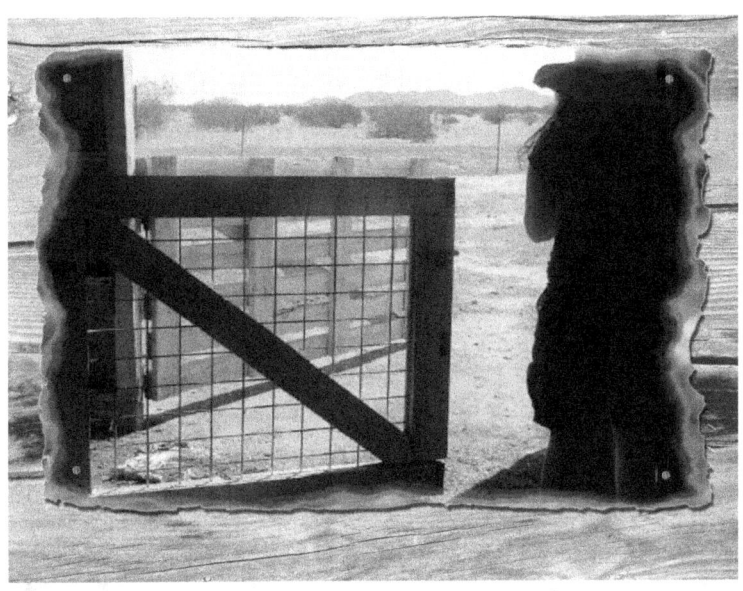

There was no romance when he stared at the desert he loved. He saw land; lots of it. It put a large space between him and others and gave him privacy and sanctuary. So long as he couldn't see anything more than a telephone pole in the distance, he was in heaven.

One of the horses neighed, but his mind was so focused on the disruption in his normal daily pattern, that the man stepped outside into the warming day and turned his face up to the sun. His wife would be aghast if she saw him not doing his usual work. It wasn't at all like him to just linger in leisure. It felt strange. Beside him, his fists were still clenched in anticipation of lifting the buckets of oats, as if his body remembered the routine, as well as his mind.

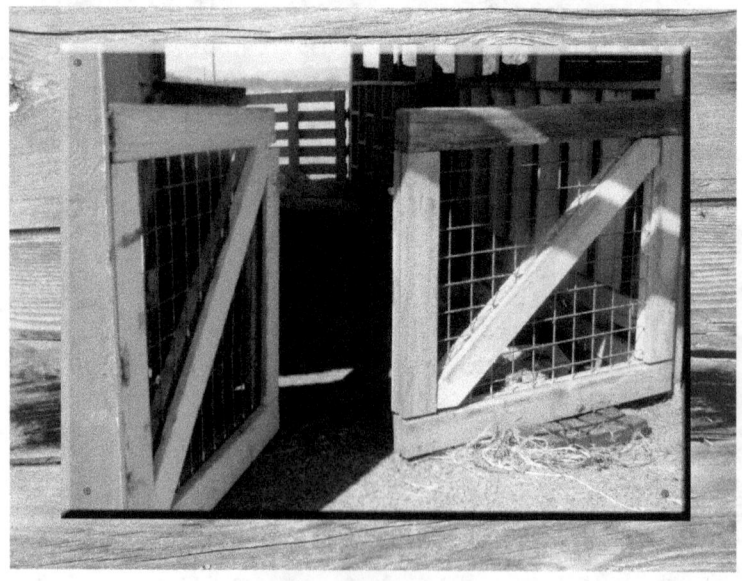

The horses neighed again.

The man shook himself from his revelry. It wasn't even like real revelry; it was more like standing vacant-minded at a crossroads. Going

Abandoned Places: Abandoned Memories (Desert Edition)

and visiting his in-laws was not unpleasant, but it meant being idle. There were no chores to be done. They kept everything in good repair and were insulted if he offered to do some task. Instead, he would sit there uncomfortably as the conversation drifted around him while his mind remained on his ranch house.

Life was tasks; one after another. The reward was in the doing, the movement, the forward motion. Sure, he repeated the same days over and over again as if the last one didn't count, but that was the same as breathing and eating and sleeping, one had to continue the cycle to stay alive.

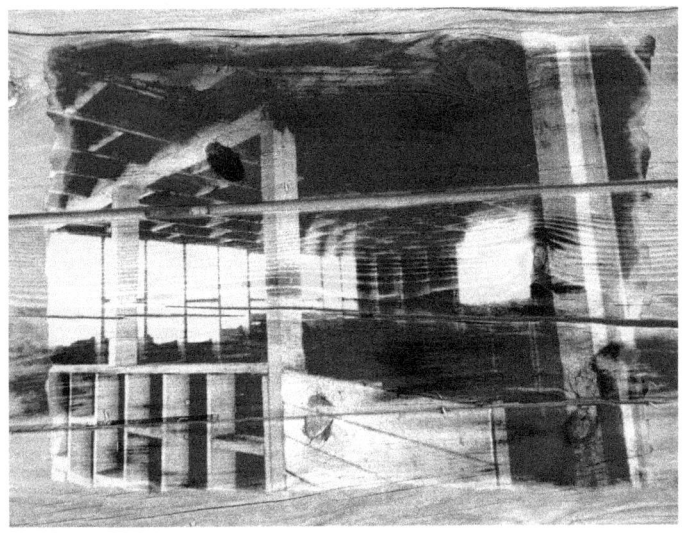

Abandoned Places: Abandoned Memories (Desert Edition)

The bright light overhead washed out the colors from the landscape until they were pale imitations of green, brown and purple. The desert looked as weary as his body felt.

He straightened up, his spine making popping sounds again as he put his hand to his low back and headed towards the stables again. The dark haven beckoned him, the smells engulfed him and the sounds comforted the man of the family.

He may not possess any sentiment, but every day his family knew that he did what had to be done and they could count on him, just like the desert sun that arrived every morning brutally early and remained until late in the day. This was how he showed his love.

This was how he lived his life.

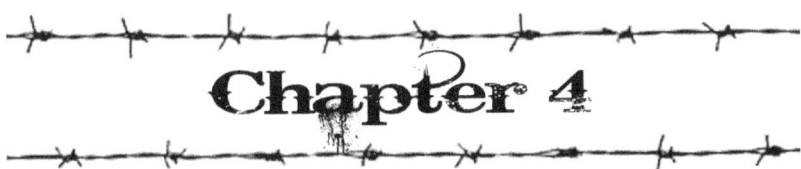

Chapter 4

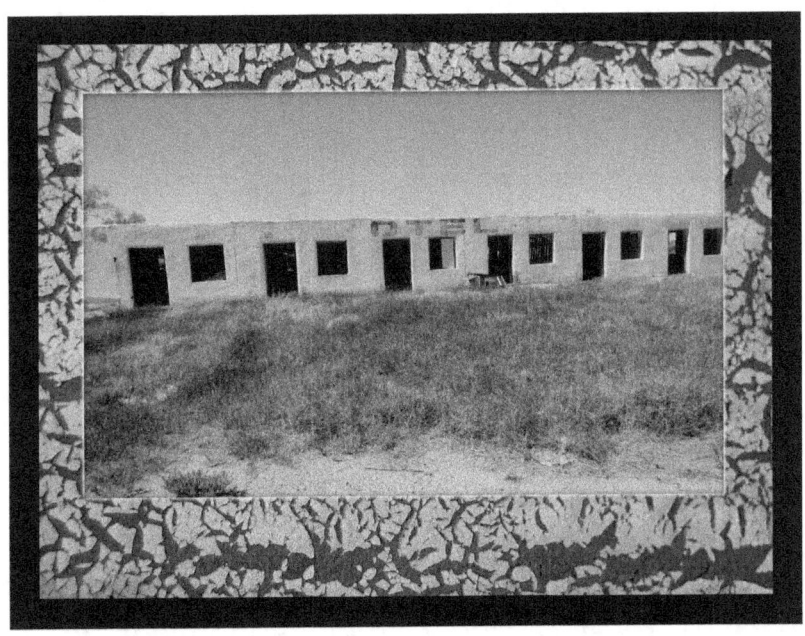

"The Angry Passionate Couple"

Abandoned Places: Abandoned Memories (Desert Edition)

This motel sat on the edge of town, completely forgotten, broken down, without windows or doors, picked over by every curious passerby. The parking lot was a mixture of sand and desert dry brush. Nature had taken its toll on the sad little structure, leaving it exposed and bleached like the bones of a whale on a deserted beach.

So, what does one psychically read in such a site? Finding one object in the disarray kept Sharon wandering around until a simple metal doorknob held valuable information.

Upon touching it, she looked up and viewed the room in the layout it once had in it heyday. This is not unlike when a person returns to his childhood home and looks past the new wallpaper and furnishings to recall the original layout.

The perspective of psychic visions is much like memories. Sharon looked around the barren space to "recall" a slender middle-aged woman with dark roots and bleached hair standing at the head of a bed, dumping a large purse's contents onto it.

Sharon sensed a brown-haired average-built man at the end of the bed, fists on his hips in a typically argumentative pose.

Pushing a little further, the names popped into Sharon's head easily. Names are not always a simple thing to attain, but upon occasion a couple uses their names in a manner that catches her psychic attention. In this case, the names were spat like curse words rather than endearments. Sharon narrowed in on "Joelle" and "Mike" and a relationship built upon sexual passion and angry chaos.

This is their story.

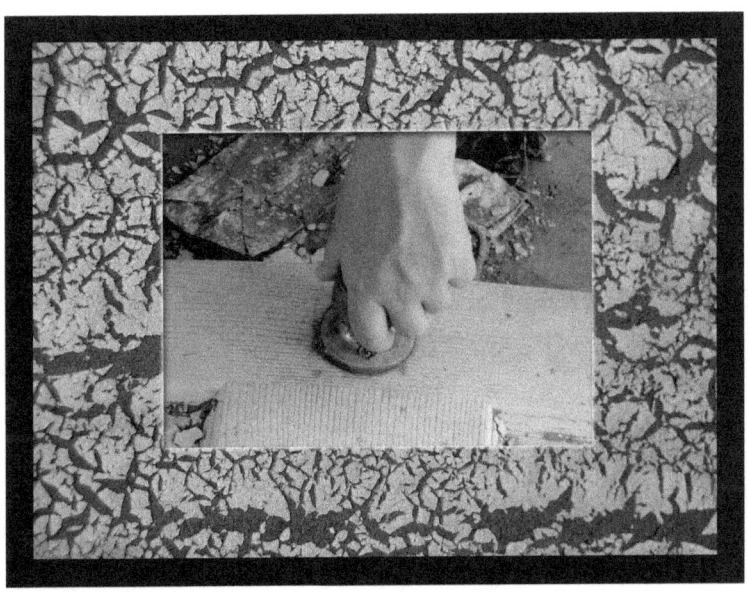

Abandoned Places: Abandoned Memories (Desert Edition)

Abandoned Motel

The slender bleached blonde dumped the contents of her massive purse onto the motel bed. The harsh desert light shone in, creating dust motes and clouding Mike's vision of the loot.

Joelle was very adept at shoplifting, but her choice of items to steal was like the men she slept with; indiscriminate and purely based on a whim at any given moment.

Apparently, today she raided a Circle K on the aisle filled with cat food, can openers, paper cups and tin foil.

"What the hell is this shit?" Mike tossed aside a bottle opener.

Joelle slid down onto the bed and sighed, leaning against the headboard and studying her afternoon's work. She bit her lip and looked up at him with big pleading eyes.

Abandoned Places: Abandoned Memories (Desert Edition)

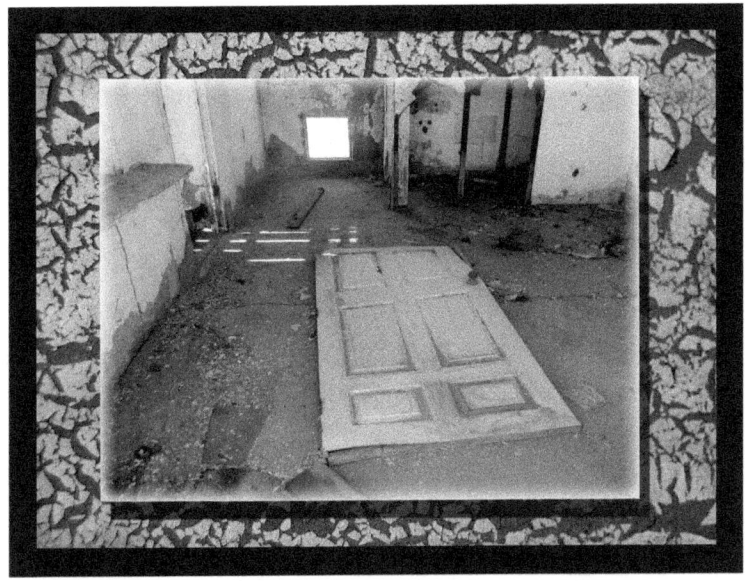

Mike ran a hand through his hair and took a slow breath. He could swear the woman wasn't 42. She seemed younger than his 29 years any day. Sometimes, she was so childlike he felt responsible for her and that did not sit well with him. He entered this turbulent relationship with the assumption that she was older, wiser and had a plan.

"Baby, we can't do shit with this!" He tossed aside a chewy dog bone. "Why would you pick that up?" He gestured.

She shook her head and looked down, her dark roots showing. "I don't know. I just wanted to get a dog." She sighed.

"A dog?" He chuckled hopelessly and got up, pacing the floor and testing the air-conditioner again. God, he hated the fucking desert! Why had he let this woman pick him up in a bar in Houston and have him zigzagging the Southwest with some promise of going to California? It had been four weeks and they were plenty close enough in Arizona. Why was she putting it off?

"We're living in a ratty motel and you want a dog?" He snorted.

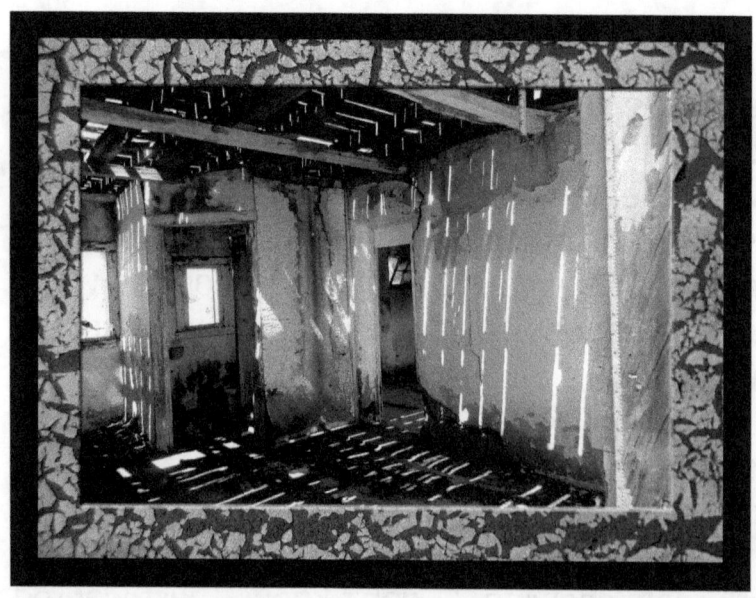

Abandoned Places: Abandoned Memories (Desert Edition)

It wasn't until her silence alerted him and her narrow shoulders shook that Mike realized she was about to crash again. Joelle never admitted she did coke, but it was pretty obvious. She'd almost gotten knifed in an alley behind a bar in Albuquerque doing a deal. It was one of the first signs something about her was broken inside.

He was drunk out of his skull when he met her in a bar and his impression was that she was on-the-ball, had a plan, was hitting the road and starting a life as an actress in California. When he sobered up, he had his doubts, but the sex was so great, it kept him following her from small town to small town.

It wasn't just the coke that worried him. The woman also drank too much, smoked nonstop, and was a serious klepto, but he didn't mind that aspect because sometimes she got them some pretty good loot. Today, however, it was time for her to crash. He saw the signs.

They'd overstayed their welcome at the little motel in the middle of the Arizona desert. Their bickering and loud sexual escapades brought the manager down nightly to pound on their door. There also was apparently nowhere for her to score her drugs, so she was drinking more than usual and remaining in a constantly depressed state.

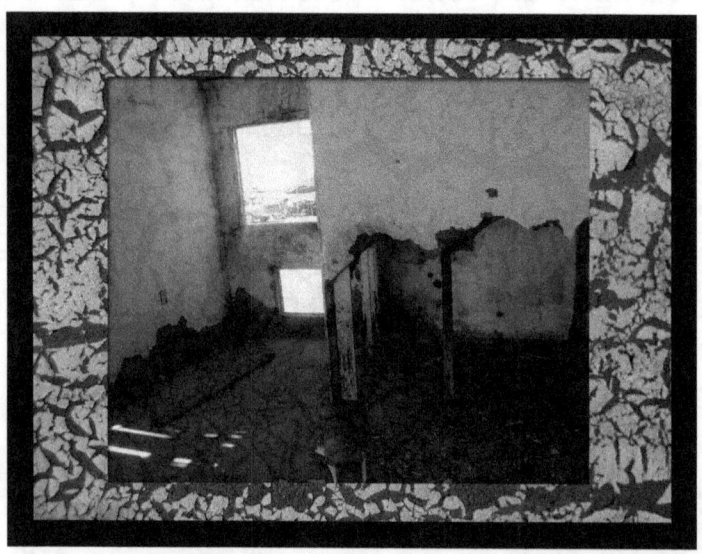

It didn't say much about Mike that he hung on, but there was nothing back in Houston but a shitty part-time job and his mother's basement. California sounded like a fresh start, even if he had to live with Joelle for a while until he could find his own independence. One thing for sure, he wasn't staying with her crazy ride through life. He may have been wasting time, but eventually he really wanted a normal life. Whatever the hell that was.

Abandoned Places: Abandoned Memories (Desert Edition)

"Hey," he put his hand on her bony shoulder. "Whatcha say we got to California now instead of waiting to hear from your friends there?"

She put her head in her hands and her narrow shoulder shook harder. He couldn't hear the muffled reply.

"What? Joelle? Joelle?" He pulled her hands from her tear-stained weary face.

"We can't go to LA." She sniffled.

"Why not?"

She pulled out a cigarette and lit it, taking a few fast puffs and sniffling before she replied. "Because there's nothing there."

He snorted. "What, the town is gone?"

She tossed the lighter at him. "No, you ass! There's no one there to meet us; nowhere to stay. I exaggerated. They weren't my friends. They're my cousin's friends. We used to talk about going there and living in an apartment and working as actresses."

He sat down on the bed, pushing aside her stolen loot. "What happened?"

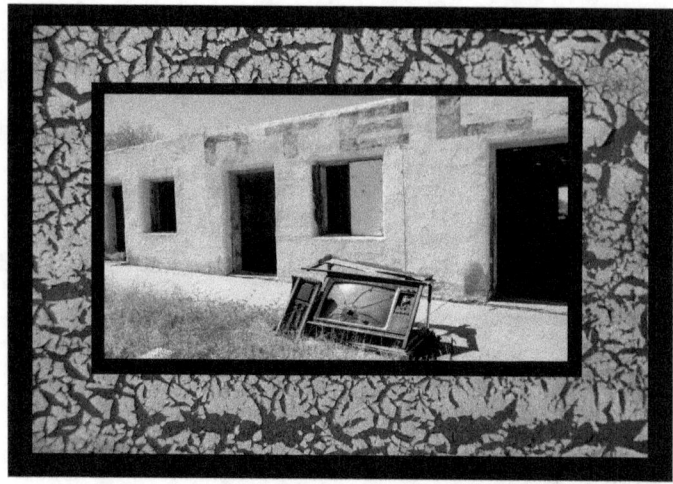

"She got married and pushed out a bunch of babies. We never went to LA. It was just a stupid dream. Everything is just make-believe. Nothing is real." She squashed the cigarette out on the night stand, parted her long thighs and pulled him down atop of her.

"What do you want?" He murmured as she arched up against him. Mike cupped her breast. He knew when Joelle needed to feel something and he'd rather it be arousal than depression. Besides, this was what kept him coming back again and again. She was insane as a celebrity on pain pills, but he did know she satisfied one aspect of him that tended to make all the decisions for him; his sexual needs.

Abandoned Places: Abandoned Memories (Desert Edition)

Chapter 5

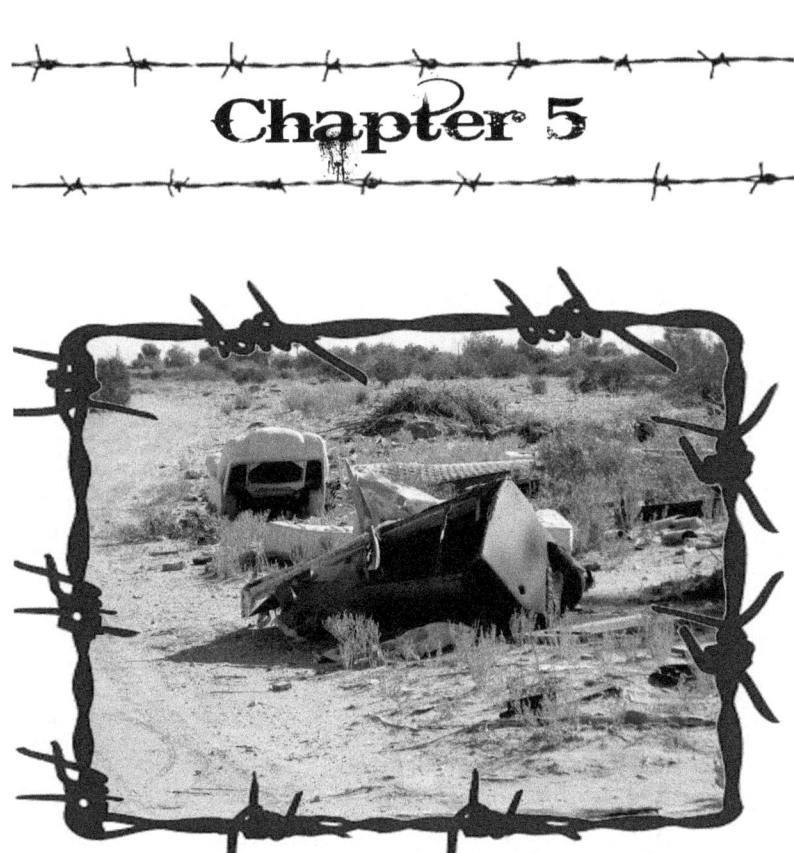

"Invisible Annie"

Abandoned Places: Abandoned Memories (Desert Edition)

We stopped on a dirt road on our way to an abandoned structure when we saw a disarray of trash on the desert floor.

Sharon pulled over and Julie joined her to inspect this makeshift dump. Sofas, mattresses, toys, bags, tools, clothing and more filled up an area of about a half acre.

Intrigued, we sifted through the finds. Under a large tree, someone had made a lean-to shelter protected from the sun by box springs standing on end and mattresses and pillows on the ground with lots of empty water bottles spread out across the powdery dirt.

Sharon shook her head and wandered until she felt the need to stop for some reason. Something was calling to her, *but what?*

Amongst the debris at her feet, she spied a doll face down in the dirt. She lifted it up and studied its completely worn face.

One name came to mind immediately.

"Annie."

"Were we planning on using this location?" Julie asked.

"Yeah, I think so." Sharon's voice trailed off as she opened herself to the information that Annie held. Even in the unrelenting sunlight and harsh pounding monsoon rains, the doll still held a lot of information. In fact, Sharon decided to keep the doll for her abandoned doll collection and the doll's name would be "Junkyard Annie."

Although Annie's owner had nothing to do with the site, her doll still held information about the little girl. In fact, Sharon was unsure if the doll or the girl was named Annie, so she referred to the girl as "Invisible Annie."

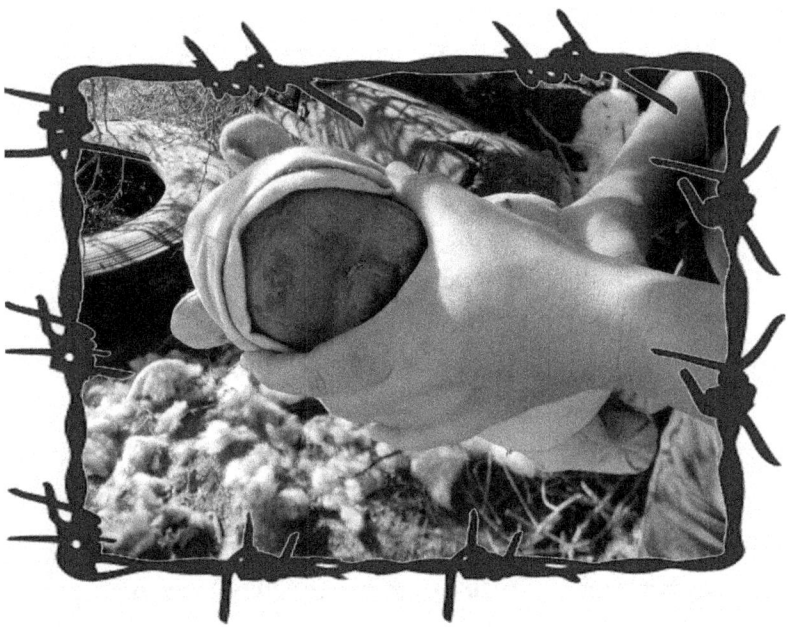

Abandoned Dump

The first years of the Annie's life were golden. Her parents were not the best functioning human beings, did not make the most money and often times argued, but for Annie, it was her world. All attention was upon her.

It was that way until "he" appeared when Annie was 3.

He was a little boy. He was an irritating bundle of screams and drooling, barfing and pooping. Annie couldn't understand why he held so much fascination for her parents. Their voices changed when they approached him, but they spoke to her like a little adult.

And, a little adult was what this 6-year-old had become and all because of *him*.

Annie could not even get mad at him because as the boy developed, it became obvious he was not speaking when he should, was not progressing normally. He had tantrums and frustrations, could not play with her without causing a scene and more often than not was in her mother's arms for the greater part of the day.

Abandoned Places: Abandoned Memories (Desert Edition)

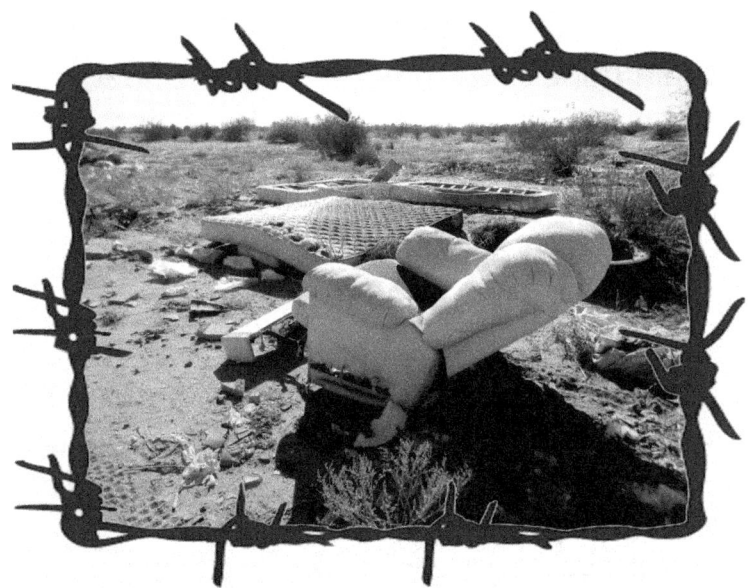

Her father came home and didn't smile at Annie and swing her upside down anymore. Instead, he asked how her mother was doing and then hoisted the boy up onto his shoulders and talked to him, even though the boy did not respond or seem to appreciate the attention.

She held up her latest drawings, read something from a book, showed him a dance she saw on TV; anything to get his undivided attention. Her father smiled at her, but the look in his eyes was distant and Annie realized he could not tell her what she just said or did, it had not registered.

Abandoned Places: Abandoned Memories (Desert Edition)

Her mother enjoyed girlie things like ruffles and hats, dresses and pigtails,
so the girl buried her tomboy ways to show an interest in dressing up in her mother's clothing. This temporarily drew attention to her and got her mother interested in taking her shopping. It was something they could share without *him*. Well, at least she assumed that, but the girl learned that was not so. Her mother was the only one to be his caretaker. Taking him into a mall was miserable. He had to wear a leash like a dog and burst into frustrated tantrums because he hated new places and new people.

Something happened when Annie started first grade. Her first papers came home with stars on them and her mother laughed in delight and excitedly called her dad to tell him of her achievement.

Annie learned quickly that her parents counted on her to get an education, to do things *he* could not. Her role in the family was assured and her shelves were filled with books and a doll in her arms that she read to. If she wanted her parents' attention, she had only to read a passage from a book or ask for help with studies.

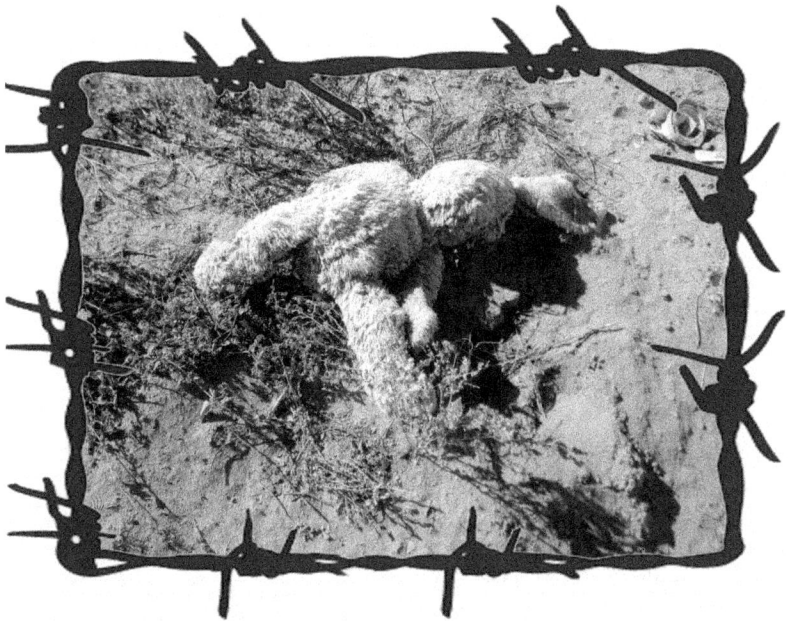

They pressed new responsibilities onto her little shoulders and Annie eagerly performed them, looking to the approval in her parents' eyes to know she was important. The only chore she wouldn't accept was watching *him*. His tantrums became worse as he approached 4 and her mother often times looked tired and overworked. Any time the Annie could jump in and make it better, she eagerly did so. Secretly, she hated his moods but also was glad for them because they were wearing down her parents. He was no longer the one who needed all their attention, he was now the one who needed constant supervision and her parents were becoming more and more tense.

They fought more than usual lately and Annie had to choose which one to go to. Her mother wanted to be alone. Her father looked sad. She would do a dance for him or tell him about her doll and he would smile and turn on the TV and they'd watch a show together. They didn't talk, but he seemed to feel better.

Her mother would join them but not sit near her father. It didn't matter to Annie. She saw that she was the thing holding the family together and that made her feel useful. She had, after all, brought he parents together in the same room.

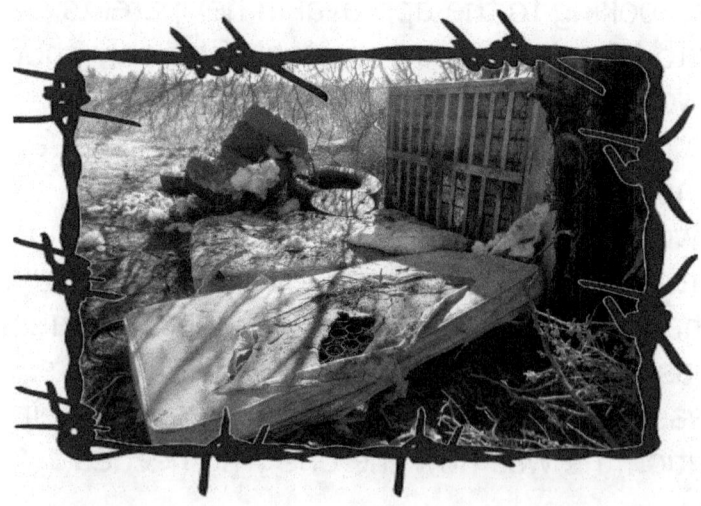

Abandoned Places: Abandoned Memories (Desert Edition)

He went into the hospital for a few days and her parents were silent. Annie began to study the moods of everyone in the house to see that his return made things feel more normal again, even if he was sitting with the same toys for hours on end, rocking back and forth and often times going on the attack. Somehow, it seemed they needed him. In fact, even she felt strangely more on alert when he was gone than when he was there with his unpredictable moods.

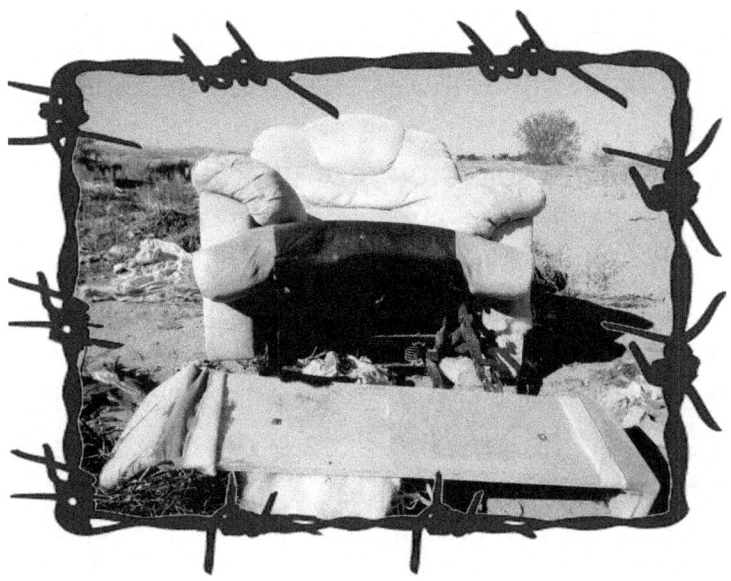

Abandoned Places: Abandoned Memories (Desert Edition)

Sometimes, she lay awake at night wondering about everyone's feelings, thinking how she could cheer them up, hoping to make it all better. Her parents argued and their muffled voices penetrated the thin walls of their home. Her father left one night and didn't come back for two days. Her mother said nothing. Annie didn't ask. *He* never even noticed.

She became more and more fearful of going to school and leaving her mom and *him* alone at home, worrying that something would happen while she was away and that if she was there, she could somehow prevent it. This magical power she gave herself soothed her anxiety. Annie just knew if she was there, just her presence would stop more bad things from happening.

She sensed her father was pulling away and becoming more distant. When he did finally leave for good, Annie should have been overwhelmed, but she was actually relieved. Her mother over the ensuing days seemed happier, smiling more, playful and fun.

It was then that Annie realized it wasn't *him* that was the problem. It was her *father.*

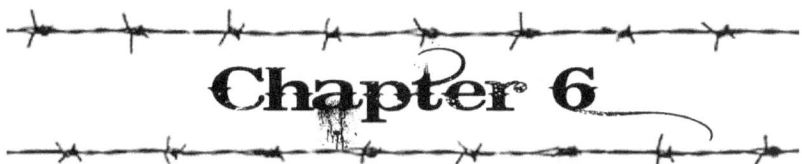

Chapter 6

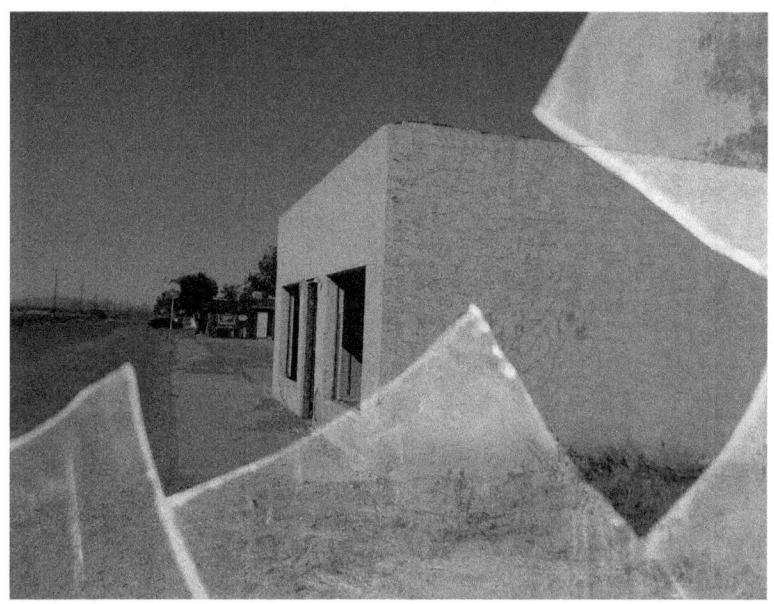

"Fighting Brothers"

Abandoned Places: Abandoned Memories (Desert Edition)

There was nothing about this beat up and hollowed out shop along a desert highway that screamed to Sharon as she drove by. It was more like it whispered. She ended up doing a U-turn, knowing she would regret not inspecting it to see why she felt compelled to investigate.

It had been stripped of its interior so long ago; it did not exude a great deal of memories. Still, with a bit of touching and prodding around, she managed to find a spot that showed immediate promise. She circled the room, touching many things that might commonly be touched and kept coming back to the same wooden post.

Admittedly, when it comes to psychometry, Sharon has found over the years that metals and stone are easiest to read especially if fairly pure, wood and glass is slightly less easy and the hardest things are paper and plastic. It's almost as if the more something is altered, the harder it is to read or perhaps the more porous it is the less it contains. This wooden beam would not have been her first choice for a read, but it did hold some active images.

It was while touching this rough wood that she looked up and images in her mind like

Abandoned Places: Abandoned Memories (Desert Edition)

memories played out of two brothers never meant to be enclosed in such a tight space.

Interpretation is the greater part of success with psychic reads. Sharon assumed these men were brothers because their roles were well defined as to who was responsible and the charming irresponsible one who never completed a task. As well, she could sense their long history together. It could have easily been that they were friends or cousins, but her interpretation was that they were brothers, as they seemed to share some similar physical features, as well.

Their age difference was significant enough that the elder felt an almost parental role towards the younger one. They were rough around the edges, from blue collar origins and neither finished college even though they gave it a stab. One was restless and had no idea who he was, a chameleon who adjusted his personality and interests to those he depended on for either a place to crash or to pay his bar tab.

The other was set in stone, certain of his values and responsibilities. He hated to be idle and he had big dreams and would never stop until he outdid his last endeavor.

This dynamic intrigued Sharon and she

liked being in the eldest's head. He seemed much more tied to this location. When doing reads, Sharon often felt the relationships around the person she was focused upon and they came to life for her as if seeing them through the memories of her target.

She went ahead and continued her read to get this scene indicative of the men's relationship. With a lack of names, she simply called them "Senior" and "Junior."

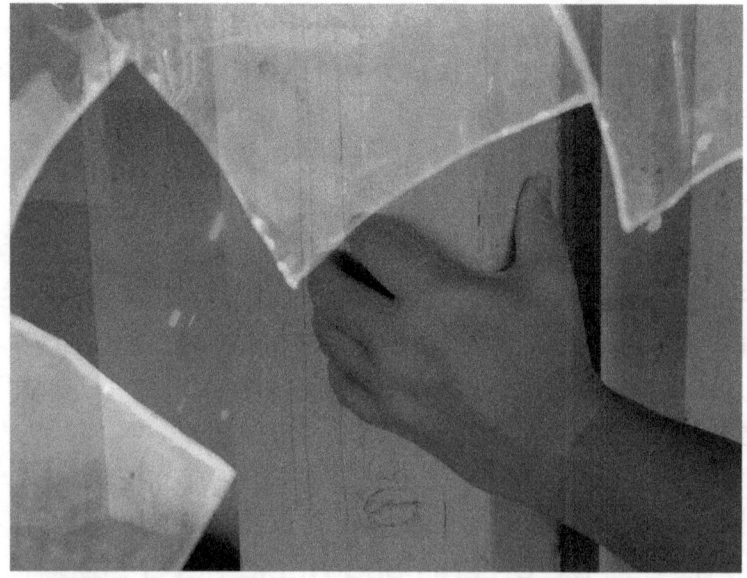

Abandoned Places: Abandoned Memories (Desert Edition)

Abandoned Shop

Sure enough, if Senior tried to pretend Junior wasn't in the room, his bothersome brother would make himself known. Because Junior needed everyone to stop and notice his entrance and embrace him happily like his posse, Senior purposely did not offer such response.

He leaned over the damn lamp he was trying to repair when his brother came up behind him and smacked the back of his head.

"God dammit!" He growled.

"Nothing ever changes." Junior sighed. "I think you were even wearing the same shirt when I last saw you." He chuckled.

Senior looked at him over the tops of his eye glasses as they slid down his sweaty nose. "Where the fuck have you been?"

"Here and there." Junior played with the cord and Senior yanked it away from him. He knew the kid well enough to realize he expected Senior to drill him with questions, but he wasn't going to take the bait. Their mother sat in adoration for every tall tale from his lips. He wasn't going to be another of Junior's hangers-on who worshiped him.

Abandoned Places: Abandoned Memories (Desert Edition)

"So, when's the wedding date?"

"The wedding date?" Senior stopped and looked up at his brother. Similar coloring and build and yet it looked completely good on him, the lucky youngster.

"You two?"

"Oh." Senior pushed aside the lamp and sighed. "We're not together anymore."

"What the fuck?"

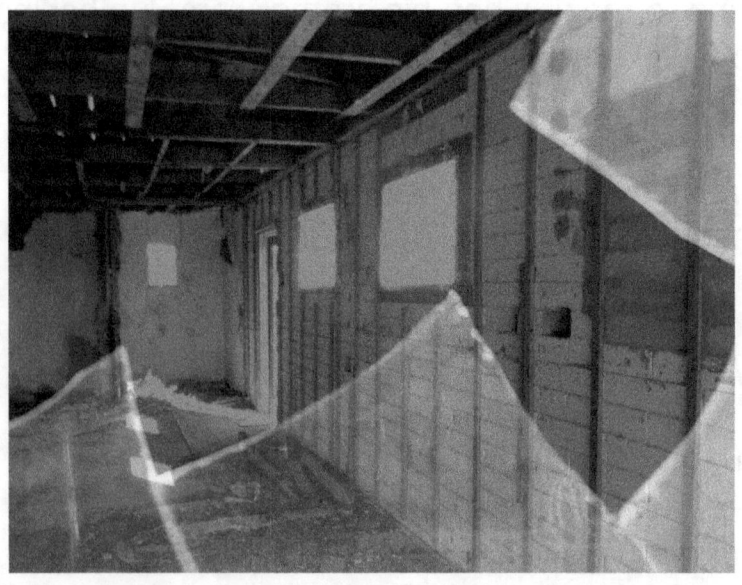

He got up and walked away but Junior tagged along.

Abandoned Places: Abandoned Memories (Desert Edition)

"I put you two together."

"You hardly put us together." Senior grumbled.

"I sure as hell did. She wanted to date me and I told her to date my responsible older brother. She was looking for someone steady. You even thanked me for giving her to you."

"I didn't fucking thank you for giving me your leftovers." He growled.

"She wasn't my leftovers. I never had her."

"You know what I mean." Senior's voice lowered as he slammed the cabinet shut.

"Well, how'd it go wrong? You two were great together."

Senior stopped and stared at his brother through the haze of sunlight coming from the window in the late afternoon.

"Hell if I know." He shrugged.

"You have to know."

"She didn't want to marry."

"You asked her?"

"Kind of."

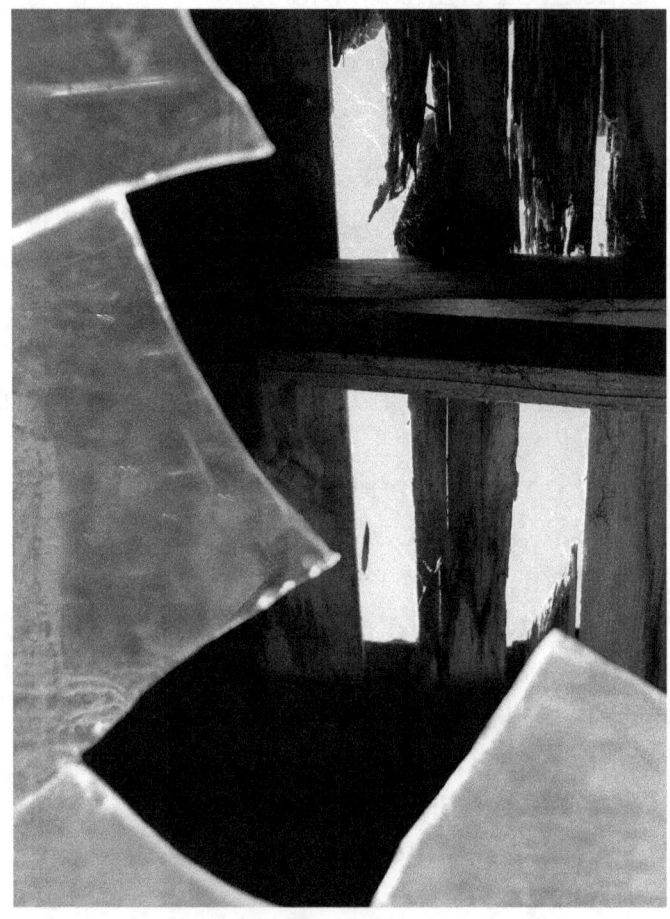

Junior sighed. "How did you phrase it?"
"I said that I was wondering where we'd be in five years. I said I saw myself being married and having a kid on the way."

Abandoned Places: Abandoned Memories (Desert Edition)

"Did you tell her you saw it with her?"

Senior ran a hand through his hair and walked away but Junior tagged along behind him.

"You fucked up, bro." Junior chuckled. "You can still rescue it. Just tell her you meant her. Come up with a fancy way to propose that she can't say no to."

"Get the hell out of my business!" Senior snapped.

They lapsed into a silence while Senior finished reassembling the lamp.

"She's seeing someone else already?" Junior asked.

"Yeah."

"Well, then fuck her! There's plenty of women out there."

"Maybe for you." Senior growled. "She was the one."

"And you just let her walk right out of your life without saying straight out you wanted to marry her?" Junior shook his head. "If you were half as ambitious about your personal life as your professional life, you'd have wedded her and bedded her and given me a niece or nephew by now."

Abandoned Places: Abandoned Memories (Desert Edition)

Senior grabbed him by the shirt and shoved his brother against the wall with a thump, The lamp tumbled from the table and his brother's eyes widened and then he did the one thing that would piss off Senior even more, he smiled. It was a knowing grin as if he were pleased he made his big brother lose it. Junior often employed that when they were kids so Senior would get in trouble with their mother for picking on his little brother.

Spit sprang from Senior's lips and sprayed his brother.

"It's my fucking life! I don't need advice from a wanderer who can't hold a job or a girlfriend."

He let him go and turned away, but he knew his baby brother enough to know he had one weak spot and that was his lack of ambition. And, Senior continually used that soft spot to give the kid some humility.

"Fucking hell! You're not pouting are you?" Senior turned around, knowing what to expect, a sulking baby brother whose party was ruined by his thoughtless outburst. He half expected their mother to come through the door and scold him with that wagging finger and sideways head tilt.

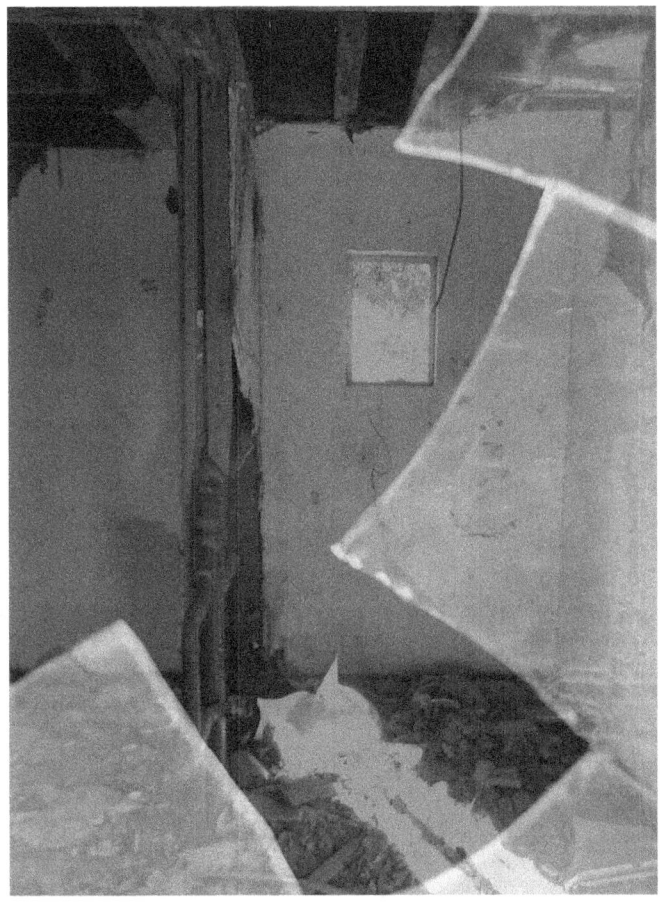

Instead, Junior was up against the wall, arms wrapped around his sides, laughing his ass off.

"What is so freaking funny?"

His brother stopped, trying to speak, but then began again with his hysterics.

Abandoned Places: Abandoned Memories (Desert Edition)

"You're a moron, you know that!" Senior muttered and walked away.

"You're really in love with her, you poor sad fool!" Junior stumbled after him.

"God, this is great! I never thought I'd see you care about another human being other than your own ambitions and what mother thinks of you. You know, mom's gonna be jealous. You *are* her favorite."

Senior pivoted on his feet. "*Her favorite?*"

"You really don't see it, do you? She brags about all your accomplishments, berates me to be more like you." Junior waved his hand in the air. "Why can't you be more like your brother? He has a plan in life. He's getting somewhere. You can't live on your charm forever, you know." He mocked in a high-pitched voice.

"She says that shit to you, *really?*" Senior was baffled by this news.

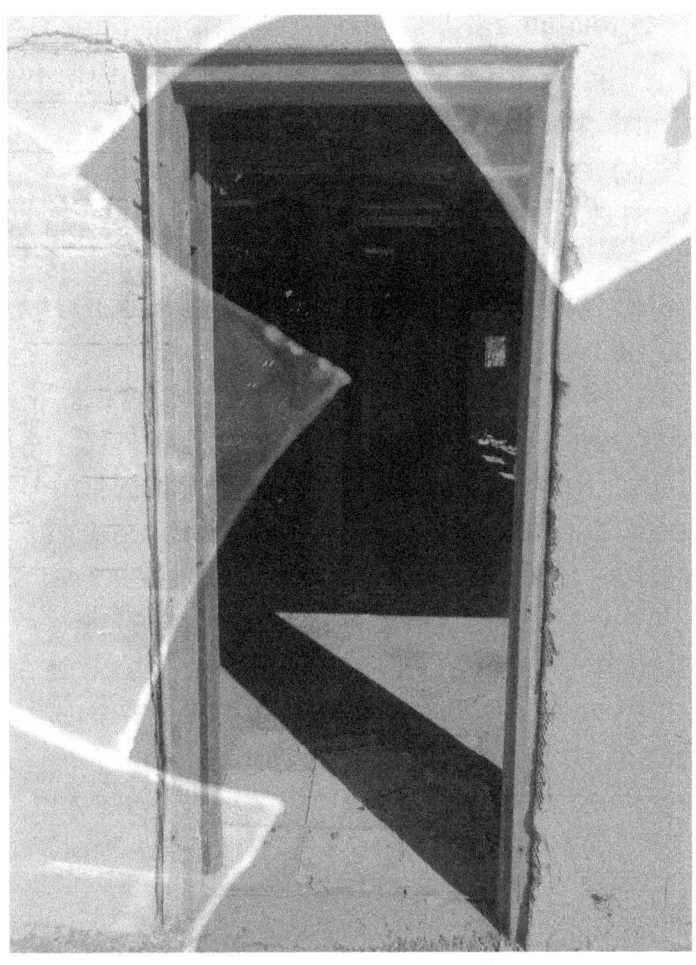

Junior sighed. "Yeah, well, she fusses over me because it's my job to never grow up and make her out of a job as a mom. *You* certainly never needed mothering."

Abandoned Places: Abandoned Memories (Desert Edition)

"Really?" Senior felt the room tilt with that insight. His brother was more perceptive than he gave him credit for.

"Yeah, well, it beats having to be overworked like you to fill out all her dreams of having a successful kid." He sat back against the desk and folded his arms over his chest and looked at his brother.

In that silent stare something clicked. They both turned away and Senior went back to his work and Junior rummaged through the small fridge to find a drink. In that one moment, it seemed as if they put each other in their places and all the tension left Senior's body as he watched his brother wander outside into the hot sunlight with a cold beer and a posse of friends waiting in the parking lot for him.

He actually felt kind of sorry for the kid.

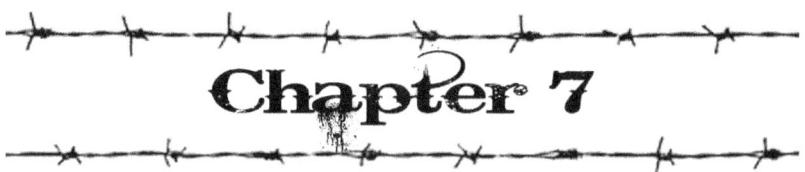

Chapter 7

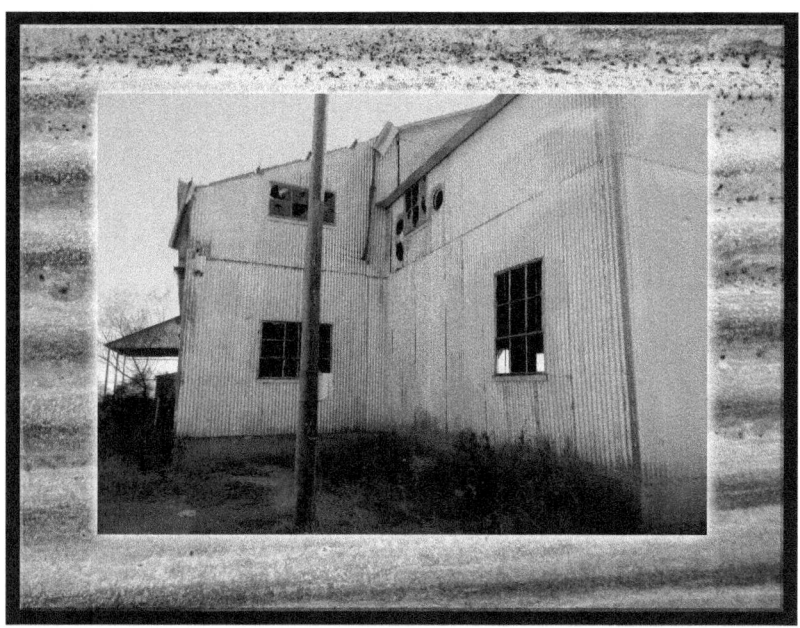

"Creative Genius"

Abandoned Places: Abandoned Memories (Desert Edition)

This location was visually stunning, a tall building set off the road with cracked windows way up high and a giant open front. It beckoned us to it just out of curiosity, but drew us inside with the sight of light filtering through broken panes of glass and birds roosting above.

The energy from this building was much like that at the abandoned factory where the teens liked to party. This one; however, had less chaos about it and more focus with regard to one young man.

There were actually many objects Sharon could read off of, but the one she chose was a makeshift table. The reason was someone was tied to that table who was a creative genius and that won her admiration.

The giant open interior of the building was tagged with graffiti and obviously a play place for small-town bored youth. There was, however, an interesting theme from a metal cage to a giant wooden box made into a mock Jack-in-the-Box, as well as clean room suits used as costumes, party favors and "beast" written on the walls, that showed a celebration occurred in the building in the fairly recent past, perhaps a month ago at Halloween.

It would have been easy to be distracted by the mayhem, but Sharon focused singularly on the feeling coming from one end of the rigged table. She felt an immediate common ground with this young man and so she let his story unfold like a recent recollection.

In this case, she got the attitude and mindset of this focus person before getting knowledge and emotional content. He had many barriers to the deeper aspects of his character and yet he was a complex young man. His self-image was built on a shaky foundation and a good deal of false bravado and arrogance. He still had a great distance to go to mature, but his drive and determination would secure his future.

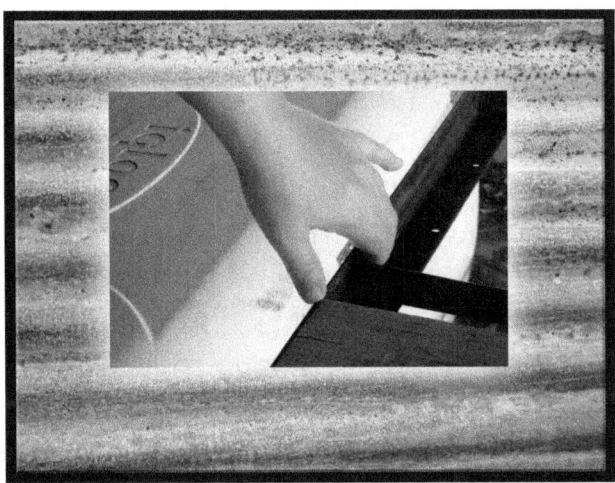

Abandoned Places: Abandoned Memories (Desert Edition)

Abandoned Workshop

He studied his "friends" cautiously. He was their accepted leader because he couldn't stand to see a group milling around and not having a purpose. He had no issues delegating and bossing folks around. He was an eldest child and that came by second nature, but more of his drive was his high level of intelligence. He was way too smart for this crowd, too smart for his family, too smart for this nothing desert town.

He played the game and lay low, not showing his intelligence or letting on that he was anything more than the shrewd leader of a band of bored older teens and the eldest in the group, in his early 20s. He worked a non-thinking grunt job and got wasted because it relaxed him, but it never slowed down his mind. One step ahead of everything, he plotted and planned how to manipulate those around him into thinking he was the shit when really he was going to cut out on them in a few months' time if things went well. The gang offered distraction until then and he didn't honestly want to have to live there for a few more months if they were pissed at him. They were not so bright, but they were powerful

Abandoned Places: Abandoned Memories (Desert Edition)

in a group and could make his life hell.

He began yet another project with the group just to get them excited and focused. In the time he'd met up with them, he's managed to get one of them working in an auto shop, another one off alcohol and into AA. They didn't realize the influences he had because the members didn't want others to know they were bettering themselves on the side, so it was his secret with each of them. Ironically, this creative genius was helping them all to prepare for when he wasn't there. He couldn't make them quick-minded and go-getters, but he could help them to see there was something else other than meeting in this dump hole and playing in the skeletal remains of a long-dead building.

He was, however, doing what he always did his whole miserable life in this nothing town, taking what he had to work with and creating something, anything to feel like it wasn't so run down, weather-worn and desolate.

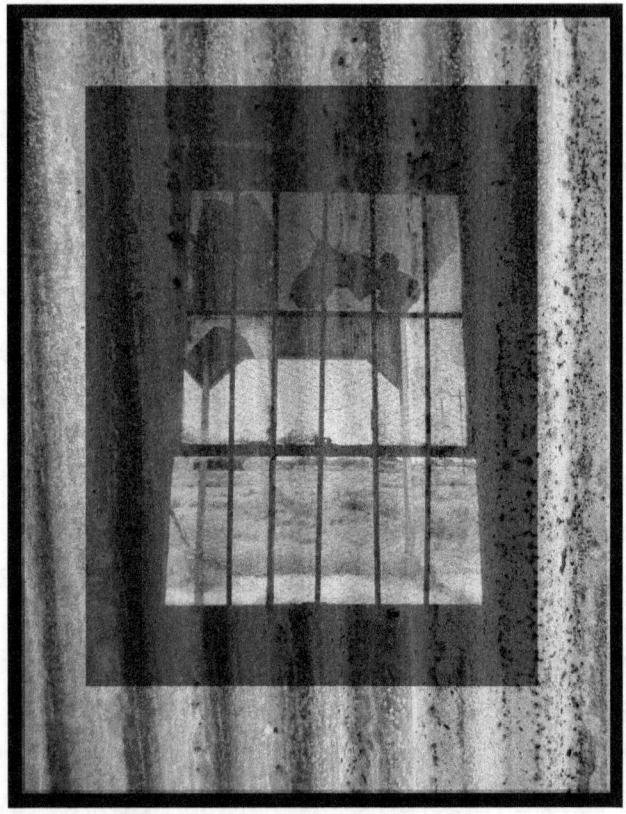

The genius was most inspired with anything left behind in abandoned buildings and dirt lots. Sometimes, it felt like treasure to him. He could find a reuse for it that would make his family marvel. He didn't get a lot of attention growing up, but whenever he fixed something or rigged something up, depending on his skill level, he got lots of compliments.

Abandoned Places: Abandoned Memories (Desert Edition)

That work ethic paid off for him. By keeping his mind ahead and working with his hands, he'd impressed people in his industry. He wanted to break away to a big city where he could use his talents to secure his future away from here.

The only thing he truly feared was being like his father and working at a grunt job all his life, becoming lame and sore and stiff beyond his years with no appreciation, no chance to be his own boss, and barely making it month to month.

No, the genius was not going to tread water. He was going to swim to shore.

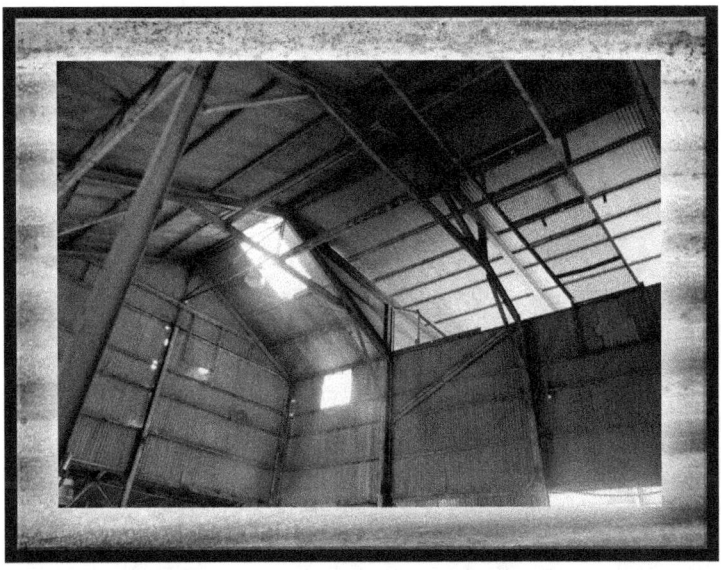

Abandoned Places: Abandoned Memories (Desert Edition)

"What will we do if someone comes?" One of the new guys asked.

"What we always say." The leader smiled.

"We were just taking a break. It's a long walk back to our homes through the desert."

That seemed to satisfy the kid who ambled away with one of the older guys.

The leader studied the group hard at work. It was amazing how without women to preen for or teachers to intimidate, the group could buckle down and focus on one task. He was proud of them. They needed to learn hard work and he'd certainly given them many of those challenges away from the streets where they'd just get into trouble.

All they had to work with was the skeletal remains of their nothing town.

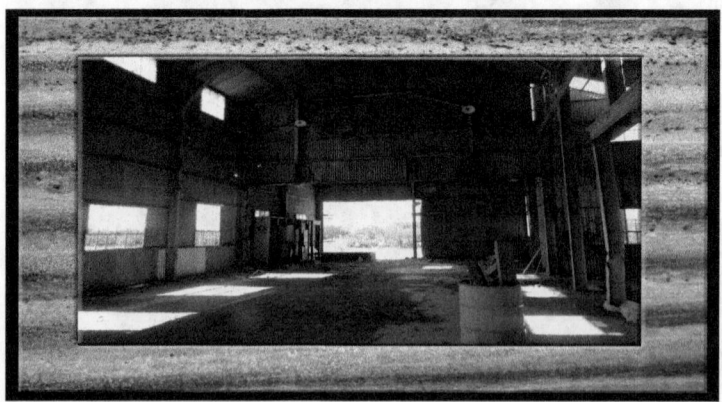

Abandoned Places: Abandoned Memories (Desert Edition)

Their playground contained rusted nails, sun-bleached boards and creaking hinges, but the nearly post-apocalyptic feel satisfied the genius. He was born into this world, grew up in, cut his teeth on abandoned sites like this one.

He hated that he had to live in such a limited place, but now he realized it made him different. He had to work his mind to focus on dreams and hopes and his abilities. Had he lived in, say, Los Angeles, he might have taken things for granted and come out of it with no skills.

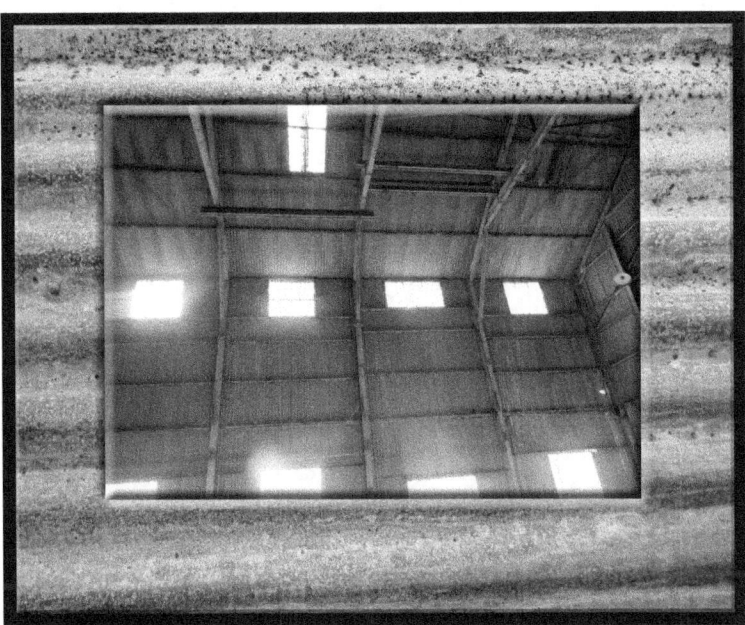

Abandoned Places: Abandoned Memories (Desert Edition)

A tumbleweed skirted along the building and the genius watched it as the dust particles stung his eyes in the opening of the tall structure. Even the plants managed to survive in this god awful desert. It meant no matter where he went, he would land on his feet.

With that thought in mind, he must have been smiling because some of the guys stopped and looked at him.

"What?" He asked.

They stiffened up and moved on with their project, knowing better than to question him.

Yes, he was well on his way to being an entrepreneur.

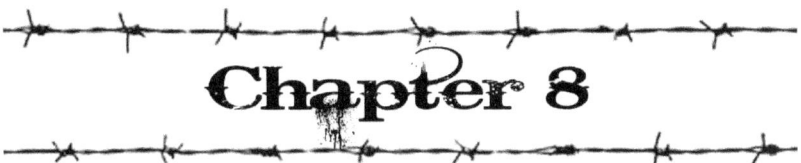

Chapter 8

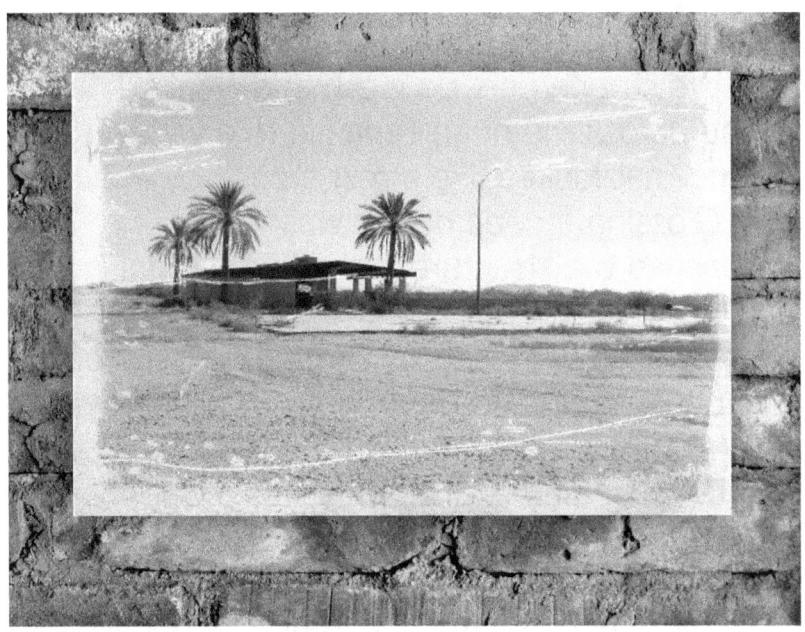

"Party Girl"

Abandoned Places: Abandoned Memories (Desert Edition)

This location was an odd one. We could have easily missed it. Back behind a resort in the middle of nowhere, a community sprang up, only it didn't exactly take off like it was intended. Empty lots sat around a few finished homes with electrical and cable boxes waiting for future risk takers to buy and build. The homes that were there looked lonely, many of them for sale.

We stopped near a wash and climbed out, looking across the huge expanse to a weird building that looked like a rest stop.

Crossing a deep desert wash, we approached the structure, revealing a tennis court with the net missing and cracks in the concrete filled with weeds. The building's doors were boarded up and the huge pool filled in with dirt. We turned and surveyed the future neighborhood and realized this was a clubhouse built for a community, but closed down with neglect.

There were so many potential things for Sharon to read that she decided to walk the grounds a few times until her feet just made her stop somewhere. Her body often times told her before her mind where a good location was. She used this technique in haunted locations for years. She would wander back and forth, her mind open, holding no real thoughts or images until she came to rest or until she kept re-approaching the same spot over and over again without any knowledge why.

It was in this part of the tattered complex that Sharon found a broken sink on the ground. She touched the faucet but her hand went to the knob. Over and over, she kept going back to the knob until she got a sense of the sex of the person and then the personality. Once she locked onto the individual, her story began to unfold. It intrigued Sharon, as the girl reminded her of herself at the age of 18 or 19, the same age as this young woman.

This party girl's story developed over time as Sharon concentrated on the woman and more and more of the view of the world through her eyes became apparent. She says it often, but such reads are very much like receiving someone else's memories through their skewed vision, biases and emotions.

This girl lived her life in the future. She had big dreams, big hopes and lots of plans. Her only problem was acting upon them. Sharon felt for this girl who stood at the precipice of adulthood, having not actually lived in her own age her whole life. Being an eldest child, she grew up fast, but with her friends she tried to go beyond her years. Even now, still in her teens, her mind was in an very adult place, anticipating a future more like a 24-year-old.

For her, it seemed there was always a better place, a better circumstance and something much more glamorous awaiting her. Her friends helped fuel her desire to become something more than average. The teen's story unfolded in an encounter with her friends and family at a get together. Without a name coming to mind, Sharon named her "Brooke" as it seemed to fit her.

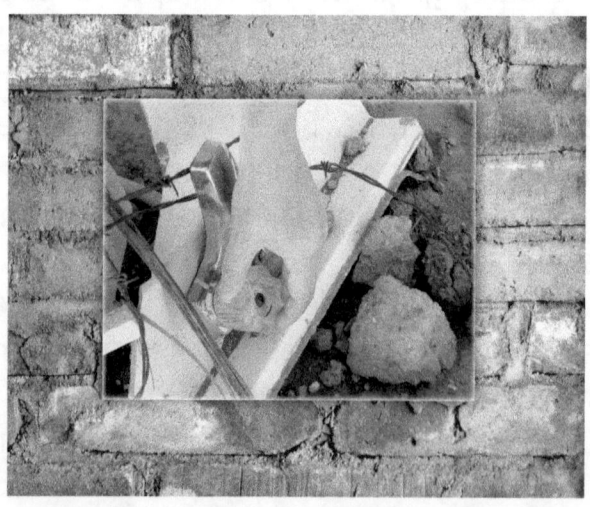

Abandoned Places: Abandoned Memories (Desert Edition)

Abandoned Clubhouse

Brooke always acted older than she was. When she was 12, she was wearing makeup, by 14 she wore high heels and smoked cigarettes. Even at almost 19, she had her head in the clouds about a fantastic future in Las Vegas.

Today, as always, she avoided a family get together like the plague, but this one offered things for the young people to do and so she went off with her friends and dodged her parents' curious eyes.

"Are you going to keep that?" One of Brooke's friends asked her.

She looked down at her sundress and shrugged. "I thought with a cardigan, it might look good this fall when we're in Vegas."

"Do you know it's cool there in September?" Her other friend asked.

"I read that you can get into any of the casinos if you're a pretty young girl, even if you're under 21." Brooke told her friends excitedly. "I am going to get a job as a dealer."

"I want to be a dancer." Her tall friend announced.

Abandoned Places: Abandoned Memories (Desert Edition)

"I'm going to be a showgirl." The other one giggled.

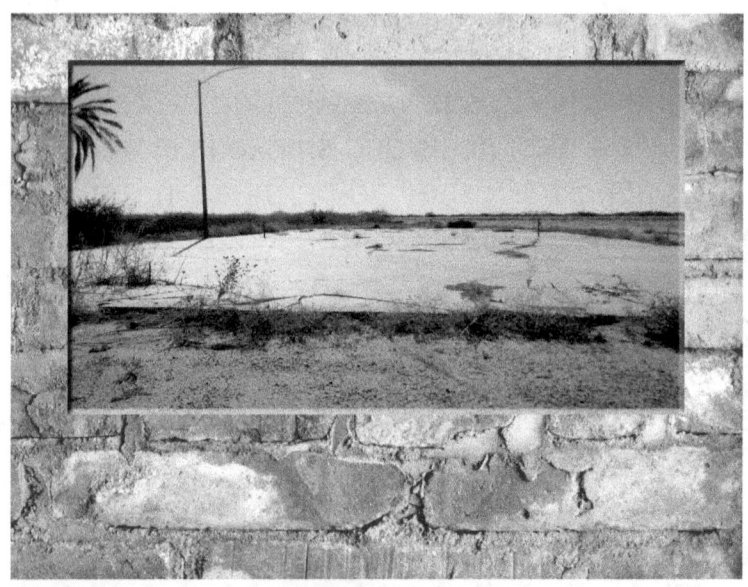

The sound of their laughter brought all the male heads to turn. The girls knew it too. They played with their hair, adjusted their clothing and lit up some cigarettes.

Being the eldest child, Brooke had to keep her image clean cut and her grades above average. Even now, she studied the groups gathered around the barbecue and looked for her parents. She left them on the other side of the clubhouse, but one never knew. She hated ruining their image of her, but she wanted so much to break away and be able to be herself all the time, not just with her friends.

Her mother told Brooke that she was only being a sheep and following her friends and their antics because the girls couldn't get into a good college like Brooke could. It bothered the teen more to realize that had wanted to go live in a dorm and make the safer transition to adulthood, but she also didn't have a clue what to major in or what she wanted to be. There was more pressure on her to do well and set a course. She had just survived high school and all the pressures. Now, she wanted the rewards of being an adult.

Her friends offered a life that meant a nonstop party, bright lights, easy money and growing up overnight. College might have worked for her mother, but for Brooke it was too boring, too safe. She wanted the risk, needed to prove herself as more than just the "smart" one.

Brooke dropped her cigarette and squashed it out as her "dream date" walked by. He watched them, but she couldn't tell if he watched her or one of her friends. Brooke hated that because she knew her friends were hotter.

One was exotic and buxom and petite, the other was red-headed and long-legged. She, however, was just dishwater blonde and neither particularly busty or curvy. She looked down at her body in the sundress and contemplated how to lose the most weight before the Vegas move. She could never compete with the showgirl types that lived there.

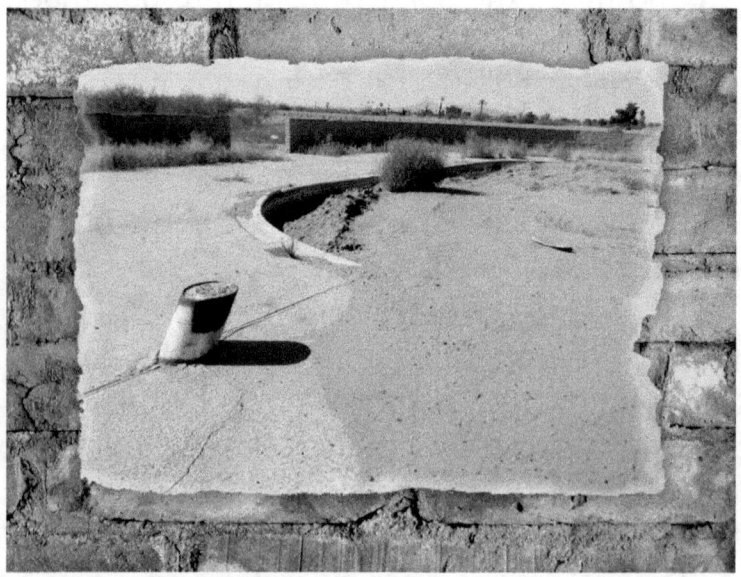

Suddenly, the dreams of the future and the lame party and the reality of her looks brought her down and Brooke suggested they go back to her house and get some booze.

Abandoned Places: Abandoned Memories (Desert Edition)

"Oh, come on. We hardly ever get to just hang with everyone." Her tall friend complained.

"Yeah, and when you drink you're a downer." Her petite friend reminded her.

"Shit." Brooke grumbled.

Mr. Handsome passed by again. She had no idea who he was. He showed up in the new neighborhood somewhere down the street from her, but she had yet to see which house he went in and out of. She just saw him walking the street or riding by in a car. He would slow down and watch her, but then she was always with her friends. Which of them was he stalking?

"Well, I'm going to the bathroom." Brooke pivoted and walked away, doing her best to stride confidently. She entered the clubhouse and stopped to lean against the building and pretend to search her purse for something, giving him a chance to approach.

She casually tilted her head back and squinted at the noisy crowd. His blue plaid shirt came into view and Brooke frowned. He stopped and said something to her two friends who put on their most interested faces, smiling up at him.

Brooke's fingers dug into her purse as she zipped it closed angrily. He was obviously waiting to talk to one of them. *Which one?* She tried to gauge his eye contact but it appeared equally connecting with both girls. However, his view was down her petite friend's busty neckline.

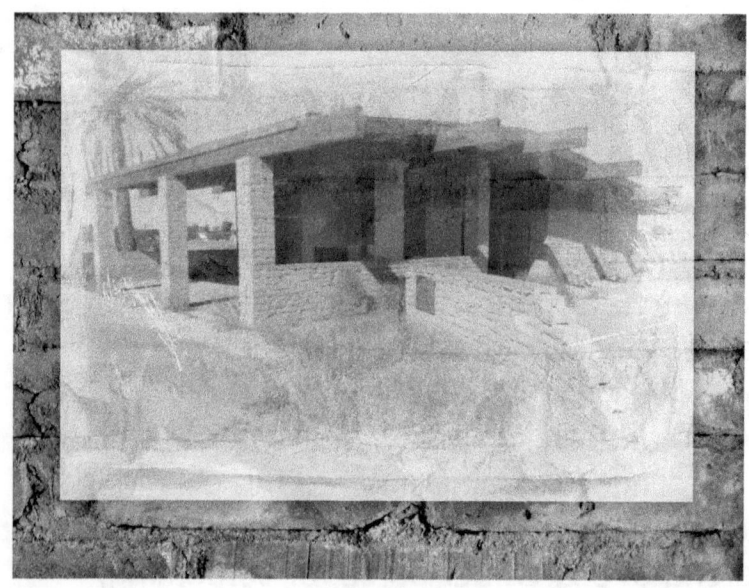

She turned on her toes and prepared to stalk back through the neighborhood to her house. Brooke's father had three bottles of open gin and not one of them accounted for in the dark recesses of the bar. She certainly wasn't feeling like a confident woman on her way to Vegas to begin an exciting life. Instead, she felt dowdy and invisible, deflated and hopeless.

Abandoned Places: Abandoned Memories (Desert Edition)

"*If you can't take competition in your friends, how are you going to take it on The Strip?*"She wondered.

This inner turmoil brought her down every time from every dream she procured. It would be her downfall. There was no hope for the future other than to go to college and take on a bogus major to make her parents happy and give her a pathway to some independence. Perhaps, if she was lucky she might get the attention of a senior graduating, become a wife like her mother did with a philosophy major that was worthless.

Her lip quivered as she stepped back out into the light to head home for that drink. A shadow cast over her and Brooke sighed, knowing it was more than likely her father reminding her she promised to stay for the whole community event.

"Brooke, *right?*"

She turned, her eyes taking in the faded jeans and the plaid shirt and the beautifully tanned and chiseled face of her dream date.

No doubt he was going to ask her for inside information on one of her friends so he can date her. Brooke had been through this routine over the past four years more times than

Abandoned Places: Abandoned Memories (Desert Edition)

she liked to count; always the buddy while the guy went for the girl he really wanted. And, she had to agonize over the guy confessing his issues in the relationship and how much he adored her friend.

Her belly clenched.

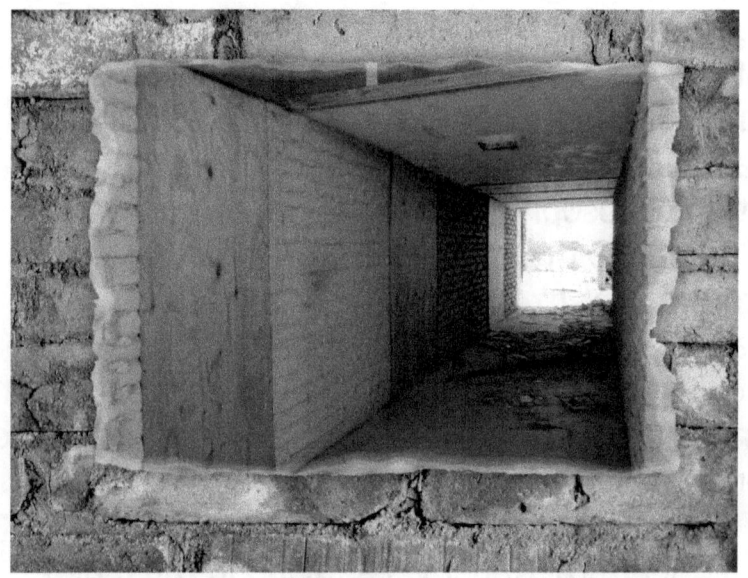

"Yeah."

"Your friends mentioned you might be wanting to have a drink. I have beers in the trunk of my car." He gestured. "It's hot. You want one?"

She nodded and looked for her friends who

were already milling around
with the other available guys.

"Sure."

"I'm Scott."

"You been living here long?" She asked
nervously as they headed to his car.

"Just temporary. I'm out of here when fall
semester starts."

"Which college?"

"UofA."

"Oh." She was going to go there if she
weren't going to Vegas.

"Your friends said you applied and got
accepted. I'm going into my senior year. I like it.
I might even go for my Master's."

They arrived at the trunk of his car,
thankfully turned away from the event where
when he popped it open, they had plenty of
privacy and thankfully shade.

"*So, when is he going to ask about my
friends?*"She pondered.

He handed her the wet cold beer and she
downed a big swig of it thankfully.

"Hey, if you're dehydrated, that's gonna
mess you up." He laughed. "So, your friends said
you're all going to Vegas?"

"Yeah." Her enthusiasm slumped as she leaned against the trunk.

He rested his hip against the trunk and watched her with his icy blue eyes. Brooke tried not to look. She had a thing for eyes and once she looked into them, she became hopelessly smitten. The best plan with this one was to keep him at a distance. He was definitely not the type that would have plucked her out of a crowd, but he was perceptive enough to recognize the smart friend who would smooth talk her friend into dating him.

"You really want to miss college?"

"I don't know. My friends are going to Vegas and I don't really want to go to college when I don't know anyone there." She finished off the beer quickly, hoping for courage as the shoe dropped.

"You know me. I'll show you around if you want to go there. I can tell you the in's and out's. A pretty girl like you might not get any studying done, though. We have a pretty big male population that won't leave you alone. Maybe you do need a guard, come to think of it." He smiled.

She blinked and looked up at him. His

eyes; they were looking at her not as a buddy but as a man, they lowered slightly to take her in from head to toe.

"*Please, God, do not let me be reading this wrong again. Surely, he's just being nice to get to one of the girls.*"

"Your friends." He began.

She sighed in frustration. Here it came; he would tell her his real motives.

"They wouldn't miss us if we walked around the neighborhood?"

Brooke blinked.

"Is that okay?" He looked insecure for a moment.

"N-no. We could do that." She admitted as he scooped up her hand and guided her towards the tract houses.

Her last glance back at her friends showed them giving her the thumbs up. Brooke's feet didn't quite touch the hard-packed ground as they walked away. Perhaps here future *was* changing.

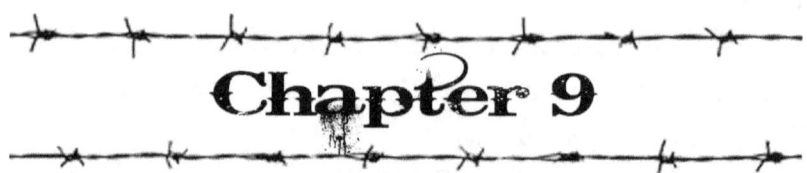

Chapter 9

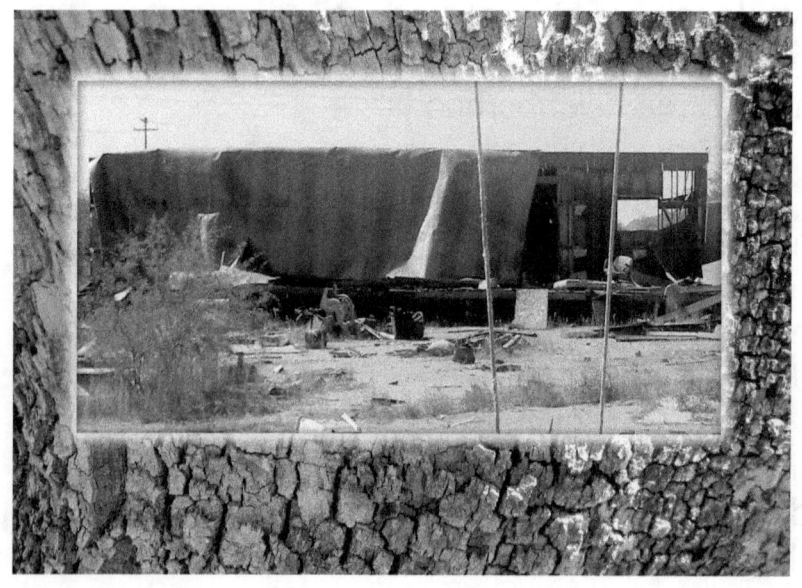

"On Her Own"

Abandoned Places: Abandoned Memories (Desert Edition)

This site was in the middle of a desert of dumped and forgotten items. The trailer was nearly completely collapsed, but it made us curious to check it out and see what was inside still. By the looks of the debris across the desert floor, we were certain the trailer contained even more interesting items.

We were right.

Edging across the rotten boards towards the door, Sharon climbed through the threshold to find it hard to enter. The place was completely stacked with items from floor to ceiling. It was actually an orderly kind of storage, but at a hoarding level nonetheless. There were stacks of lumber, furnishings including a giant headboard, a heavy dresser and cabinets and then, as Sharon turned to leave the crowded mess, her eyes settled on something leaned against the wall.

A beautiful room divider of dusty dark wood in a basket-woven pattern looked out of place in the utilitarian surroundings. It seemed like in its heyday it was quite impressive. Sharon just had to reach out and touch it.

At a time in her life of enormous change,

Sharon reacted to the feeling imbued in the wood. She was about to go through a divorce and live on her own for the first time in her entire life. The giddy excitement and complete terror combined and matched the feeling contained in the wooden screen.

As a psychic, it is very tough to not use the intellectual side of one's mind to tamp down the intuitive. When looking at the room divider, the visual of it was one of an older person with perhaps a fussy home decorated like the 50s or 60s style. The psychic read from it countered that impression. Somehow the screen ended up at that site, but before that, it was the property of a young woman.

Sharon let the woman's viewpoint enter her mind's eye and she knew right then and there who this woman was and how she dealt with enormous change. She felt an immediate kinship with her.

Her story unfolded quickly because of the emotional connection and the young woman on her own came to life in a moment in time.

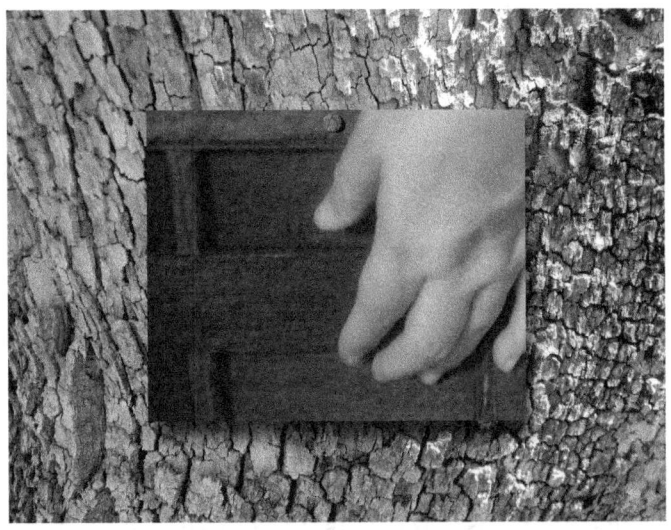

Abandoned Trailer

She stood in the middle of the large open room and spun around in place, arms open wide with joy. She had waited a little longer than her friends to make it on her own. Most of them had gone to college and that was their first time away from home. For this 24-year-old it was simply a matter of economics. She wanted to help her mother pay rent and she wasn't making much in a retail job. It was when her mother's boyfriend moved in and she was promoted to store manager that this young woman got her rewards.

Abandoned Places: Abandoned Memories (Desert Edition)

It wasn't a large apartment but with no furnishings it seemed quite spacious. She had only a bed and dresser and some dishes and cups, but family and friends were eager to chip in and give her cash for the thrift store. She had already spent several weekends coasting along neighborhood streets for garage sales and collecting all her necessary items like pots and pans, a bookshelf and an old TV.

The one thing she truly loved was the wooden folding screen she found at a yard sale and decided to use to make the one large room seem like a living room and dining room. A tiny dinette set behind the wooden screen and it would give the illusion of privacy and coziness.

The young woman fingered the ornate wooden slats and considered using it to hang her first Christmas cards in her new apartment. She smiled happily.

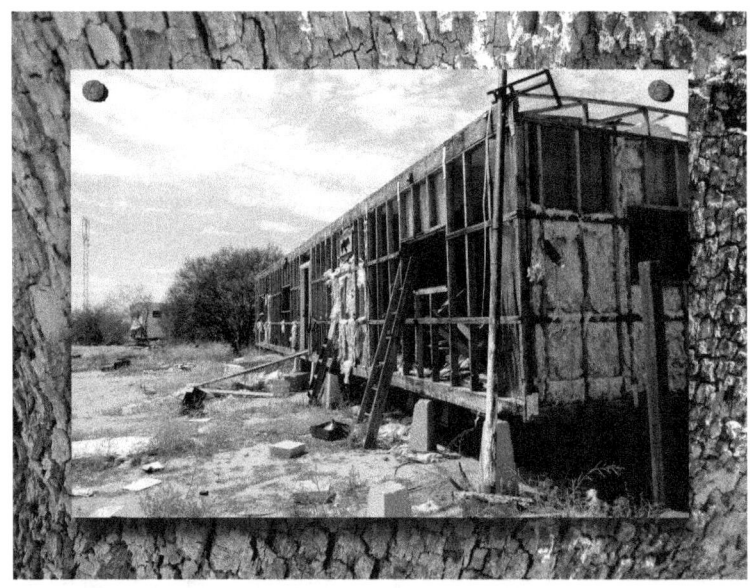

"You'll never get settled in for the night if you don't make your bed." Her mother announced.

Deflated by the sound of her mother's disapproving voice, the young woman pivoted and went back to the kitchen with the box of dishes and ignored her directive. This was not her mother's home anymore. She didn't have to do anything her mother ordered.

"Well?" Her mother asked from the doorway.

"It doesn't make logical sense, mom." She explained.

Abandoned Places: Abandoned Memories (Desert Edition)

"What? That you would want to have sheets on your bed? I hope this isn't the way you plan on living all willy nilly."

"Mom." She sighed as she placed the plates in the cabinet. "I'll be eating long before I'll be sleeping."

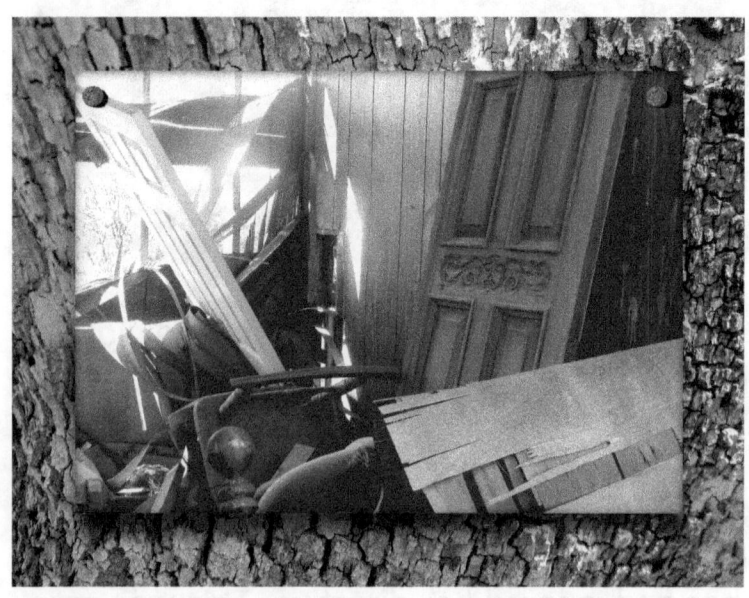

She heard her mother stalking away to the bedroom, snapping the sheets into place.

These were the sorts of battles they fought often over the past 24 years and one that she never won, but this time she had.

She smiled to herself.

Abandoned Places: Abandoned Memories (Desert Edition)

"There's no electricity!" Her mother yelled from the bedroom.

"I know." She called out. "They said they'd turn it on in the afternoon, mom."

"Well, they better." She stepped into the kitchen and began to open a box with great efficiency. "You don't want to be cold tonight. You have no blanket."

Her mother managed to make that sound like an outright insult, even though her mother was the one who told her to spend her money on a second pillow instead of a blanket.

The young woman tightened her jaw to keep from saying anything, letting her mother take over the kitchen while she left to go out to her car and get her personal belongings. The less time they spent in a confined space, the better. She learned that living with her for 24 years. Her mother was a confrontational person. The young woman could say, "I had a good day at school" and her mother would say, "it probably means you didn't get anything done." She had to say the opposite of what anyone said.

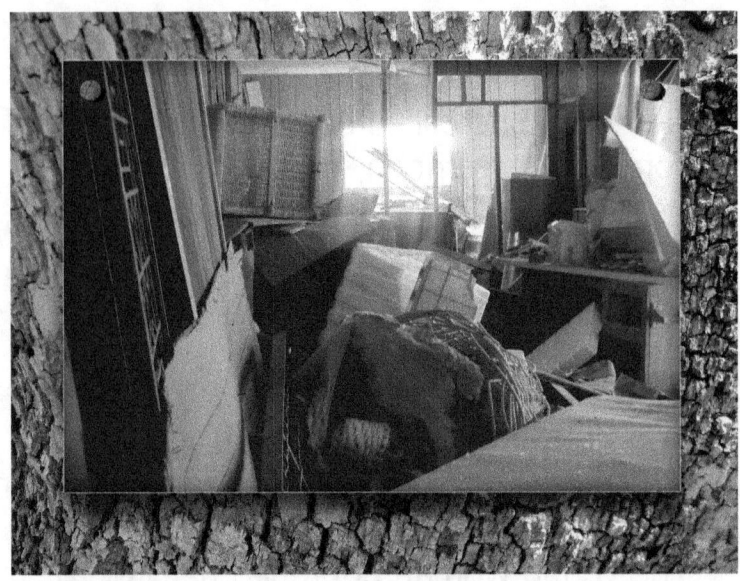

The woman's negativity was well earned. The young woman's father had been an emotional wreck and a weak powerless man. Her mother had risen to that situation and become bossier, more aggressive and controlling as if no one could be counted on to get things done.

Even knowing that about her mother didn't help the young woman. She still felt a twinge of hurt at the bitter woman's words.

She tried not to let the tears build up in her eyes as she opened up the trunk of her car. Here she was on the edge of adulthood and responsibility and her mother couldn't tell her "job well done," or "I'm so proud of you," or even the comforting, "I'm always here for you. You're not alone."

"*Hey!*"

The young woman turned to see a woman approaching her car.

"I'm Trish. I live above you. Please let me know if I clomp around too loudly." She chuckled and held out her hand. The young woman took it.

"First place, huh?" The smiling woman asked. "You were me about 20 years ago, sweetie." She laughed and grabbed a box.

"You don't need to do that."

"Hey, we have to look out for each other. Don't know about the others around here, but the apartments all around us, we're all family to each other."

That eased her tensions considerably to know that although she'd be living alone, around her there would be compassionate people should she be clueless about something or simply lonely.

They entered the living room with the boxes and her mother was nowhere in sight. The young woman knew her mother was no doubt hanging her clothing in the closet in perfect order by colors. The thought of introducing the friendly woman to her mother, even though both were of the same age, seemed a mismatch and a total disaster.

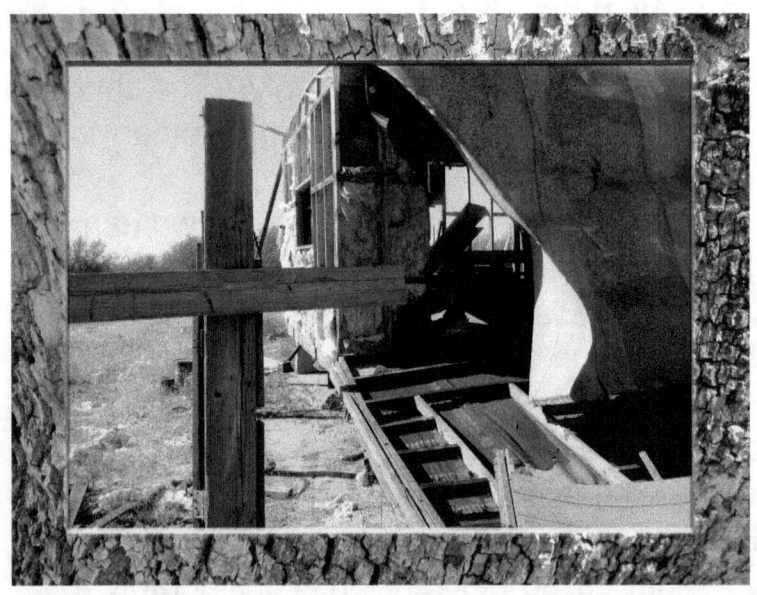

"You have your work cut out for you." The woman sighed. "I remember living in an empty nest for a time. You learn a lot about yourself when you don't have your usual trappings around you. I learned to read books finally. Never read them in school. Well, better late than never." She chuckled and patted the young

Abandoned Places: Abandoned Memories (Desert Edition)

woman on the back. "You are going to be overwhelmed for a while. Ask lots of questions. All of us went through it. I've moved on and could have upgraded to a better apartment complex, but I really like being where I first started out. It's sort of the scene of the crime. Every time I had a bad date, every time I worried about my bills, every time I got angry at work, the folks here commiserated. We have two other newbies here too."

Feeling a sigh of relief, the young woman went out to the car with Trish and got more boxes. Suddenly, being on her own wasn't about being alone, but being alone together. She liked that concept. Perhaps her mother couldn't give her that, but these people would soon no longer be strangers and be her mentors. That first night alone didn't seem so scary when Trish invited her to a BBQ in the courtyard to meet the others.

Yes, this was what she needed, to leave home only to find one.

Abandoned Places: Abandoned Memories (Desert Edition)

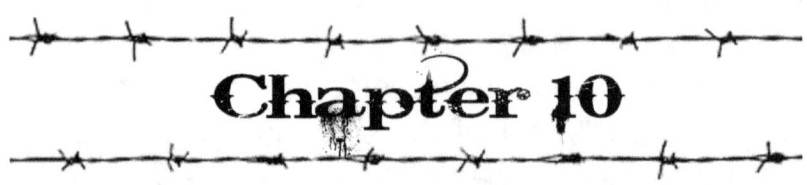

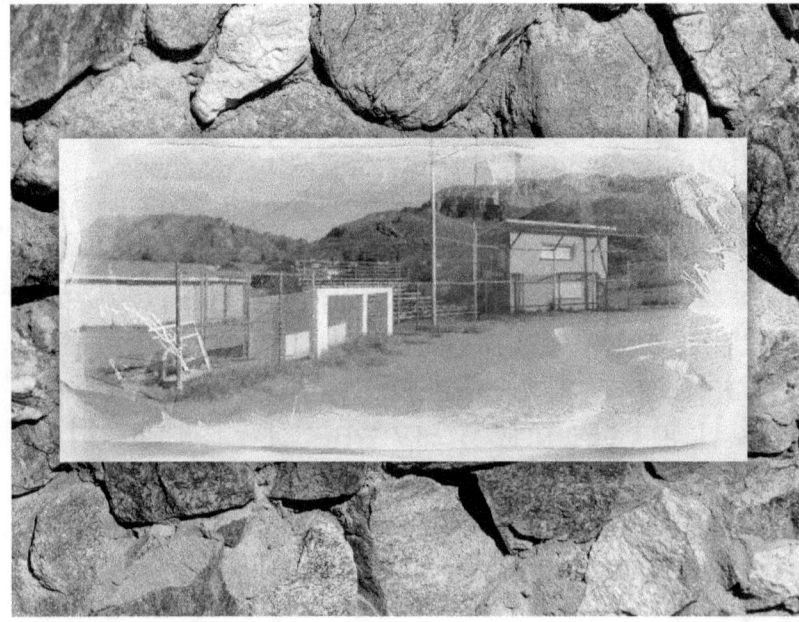

"Optimistic Ball Player"

Abandoned Places: Abandoned Memories (Desert Edition)

This site was a complete accident. We were wandering a high desert mining town when we turned down a road and ended up finding it unfold to reveal light poles. The car crept closer and soon we were parking at a baseball park.

There was no reason to consider the site as abandoned, but there was something rather vacant about it. On a plateau looking out over amazing vistas, this quiet field looked very much neglected.

We walked the field of dirt and studied the overgrown weeds. One dugout was missing its steps and was a precarious drop. The scoreboard was weather worn and rotting.

Sharon doubted it would be a good read until she climbed down into a dugout and turned around, her hand grasping the metal chain link protective fencing and an immediate emotion took over her entire body. The sensations were strong and a girl came to mind. A girl with high positive energy and her name was, strangely, *Julie.*

This girl had a way of looking at and interpreting the world around her that some would say was simple-minded, but it was really

Abandoned Places: Abandoned Memories (Desert Edition)

the mind of an optimist. The youngster sorted through all the stimuli life provided and interpreted it through the filter of "blessings." Her very outlook on life intrigued Sharon and she was driven to learn more about this little Julie.

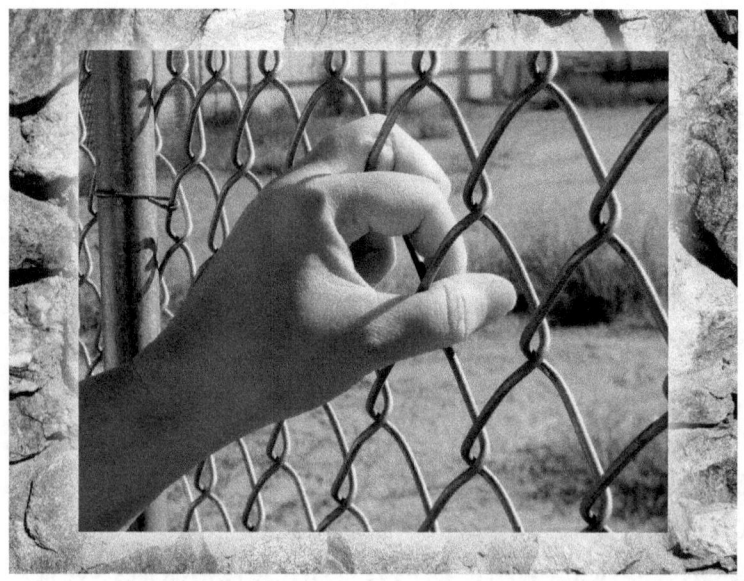

Abandoned Ball Park

Julie never thought she'd end up in a dugout or be allowed to play. Her love of tossing

Abandoned Places: Abandoned Memories (Desert Edition)

a ball was one born from having brothers and a father who liked to get them outside to play. He treated her no different than her brothers, but her interests tended to be more towards drawing and writing poems. Her father always laughed and called her his little dreamer every time the ball whizzed past her ear as she studied the clouds overhead. His patience got her here and she would go up to bat and make him pleased.

The noise, the yelling and running about distracted the little dreamer. In this fantasy, Julie was going to hit a home run and everyone would cheer. Her mind skipped over that on to the next thought and the next; the birds gathered on the light pole, the airplane trails in the sky, how she might want to draw the field and her winning home run.

That thought brought her back.

Someone yelled and Julie startled, bringing her attention back to the game. Even if she didn't hit a home run, she would have her parents watching her and cheering. For a few moments, they would be very happy to see their daughter on the field. She would make a pretty picture of it for show and tell.

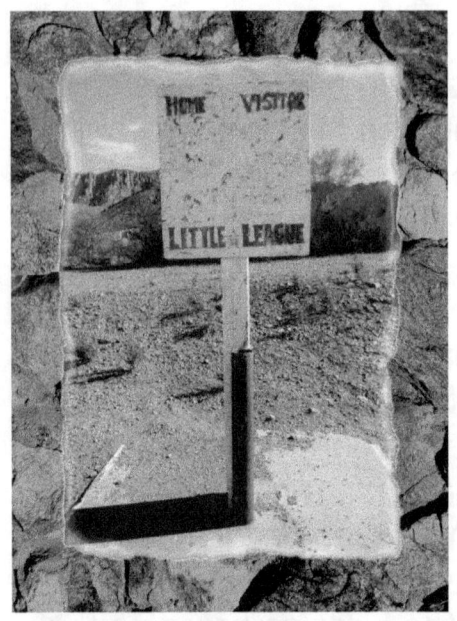

One of the kids scored and Julie screamed excitedly, her fingers gripping the chain link protecting the dugout. Everyone roared and her ears rang. The smell of the moisture in the air with a coming storm, the happiness of the moment and the way the dust puffed up in the air as the children scurried around made Julie feel a part of something really important.

Suddenly, everything her father told her about sports and feeling a part of a team made sense.

She giggled happily as one of her friends pounded her on the back. Distracted by the sight of a kid in the outfield digging at the ground with the toe of a sneaker, Julie missed her father calling at her from beside the dugout. Crouched down on his heels, he peered inside and smiled at her, waving excitedly.

Julie waved back. He gave her thumbs up and she returned it.

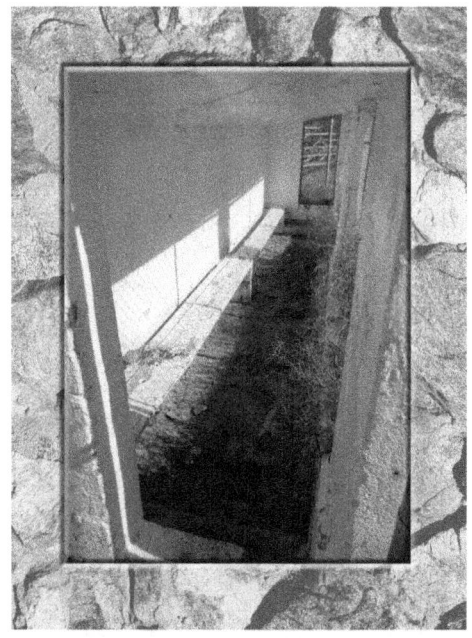

As long as she lived, she'd never forget this day. Everyone was involved in it, all her friends and her family and she had a starring role. It was magical and glowing, sparkling and if she had to call it a color, she'd choose sea foam green, no, perhaps hot apricot. *Yes!*

Julie gripped the bat and waited, trying not to be distracted by a huge bird circling overhead of the clear day that made it possible to see a distant mesa. The ball whizzed past her and she swung too late.

Focused now on the pitcher, she observed the beautiful underhanded toss.
It made a high arc and Julie swung, her bat barely missing it. Another player might have

been tense and worried about missing again and being struck out, but Julie knew that this pitcher was very good and she admired the way the next ball came at her much faster than the others. She swung too soon and it flew past her ear.

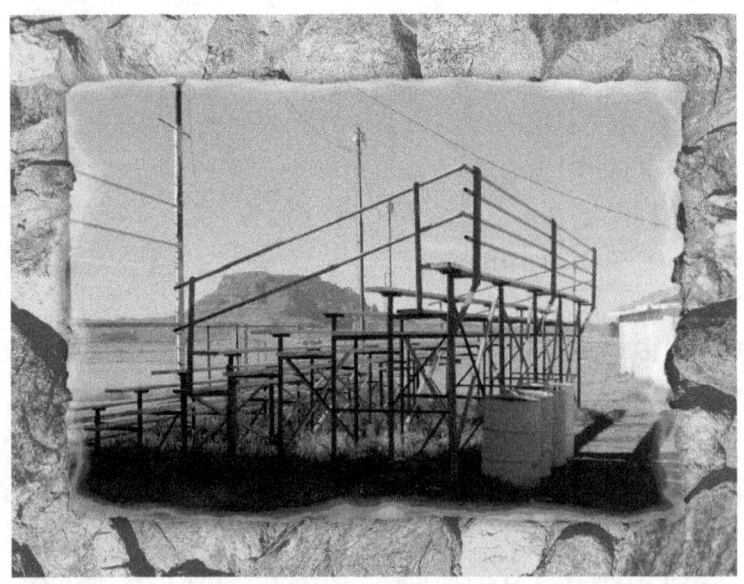

She dropped the bat and went back to the dugout as she was called "out." Her father stood up and clapped and smiled down at her as she went inside. She smiled up and giggled. He never cared about the outcome that she just played. It was perfect for Julie because she just wanted to say she did it. She knew she wasn't

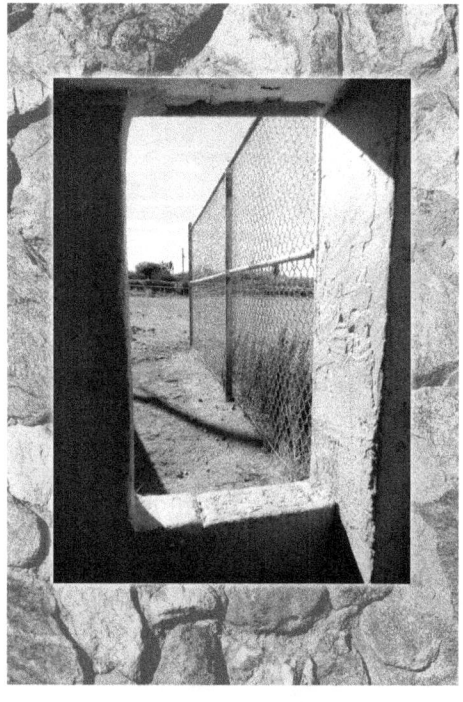

much of a player, but she was a great team member.

"You'll have no trouble with that pitcher." She told the player who was up next. "You're our best hitter." She encouraged as the player left to bat.

"You did well. I could see that your swing was much stronger." One of the parents in the dug out told her.

Julie smiled up at the woman.

"I thought so too." She giggled.

The sound of the crowd roaring brought her back to the field where the batter just made a home run. She bounced up and down excitedly, nearly losing her voice as she held onto the chain link and laughed into the warm sunlight and thought it was the most beautiful day ever!

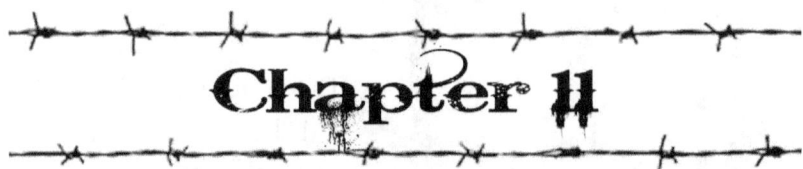

Chapter 11

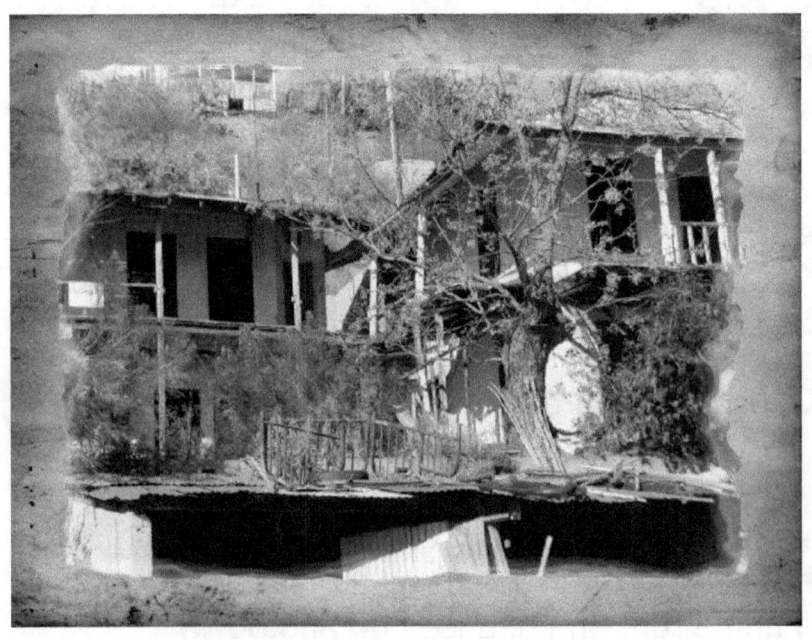

"Hard Worker"

Abandoned Places: Abandoned Memories (Desert Edition)

We wandered a hillside road, curious about the row of abandoned buildings looking down on the mining town. We stopped and studied one interesting building from its backside.

Sharon climbed down the stairs to find that they stopped and there was a big drop off. She peered into the skeleton of the house and wondered about its strange shape with walkways and a courtyard. It was for sale, so that made her even more curious what it was like. She noticed that down below there was a driveway. So, we wandered down the hillside to see it from the front side.

Sharon's eyes widened when she realized the structure was huge. It wasn't just a little house on a hillside. It was sagging, chipped away, boards curled and nasty, floors rotted out upstairs, but it appeared to be a multi-family housing unit. She climbed the concrete stairs up into the main courtyard filled with washers, dryers and ovens pulled from the apartments.

A buzzing caught her attention and Sharon stopped short and turned to see a swarm of bees under the balcony, flying in and out of the broken floor boards that bulged from a massive honey bee nest. Knowing that killer bees were the majority nowadays, she slowly backed away and went downstairs to the storage room.

For some reason, this place just sang to her. Knowing that so many people had lived in such a small space, knowing that their residual remained, Sharon's hands curled in tension. She wanted to read it all, instead, she had a storage room available. So, she took it.

The little basement-like room was barren, stripped away of its belongings, but in a little closet with a wooden bar, Sharon found something to pick up. The woman that came to mind did not present a name, as it seemed as if it was not something she identified herself with and others rarely used because they didn't know it. She was so anonymous; in fact, Sharon decided to give her a name. She called her "*Rosalita.*"

The woman was closed off to the world, but inside she was rich with insights and judgments, right and wrong, black and white and other cognitive distortions that made her a nervous bundle of energy and industry. Because "Rosalita" did not want to draw attention to herself, she had learned to not exist in public and it had begun to rub off in her private life, as well. *She existed, but did she thrive?*

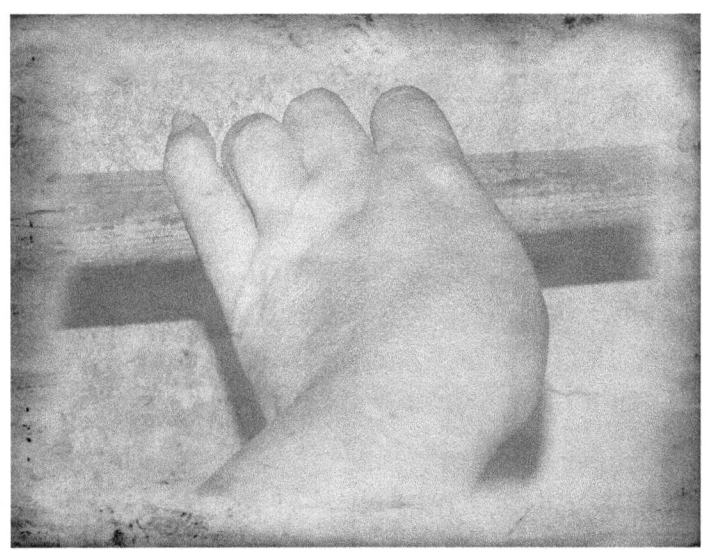

Abandoned Apartment Building

She strode along the walkway in perfect even efficient steps. Someone came out one of the doors and didn't even glance at her. She was used to being anonymous. Rosalita liked it that way. People took time out of her schedule. She knew too many men who gathered like old women and gossiped and chatted for hours on end, not getting any work done. They were a

Abandoned Places: Abandoned Memories (Desert Edition)

disgrace.

She took the stairs and watched for upcoming tenants as she looked around the box in her arms. She easily rested the box against her hip and used her free hand to open the door to the storage room and hoisted it in and set it upon the floor.

It was time to go into town and she looked forward to that. The walk down the hillside and back up again gave her vigorous exercise, cleared her mind and allowed her to get away from the crowded building.

Someone went past the storage room and she heard voices chatting. The residents stopped just outside the door and she could hear their entire conversation. Rosalita never drew attention to herself, so she would not go out there and let them know of her presence. Instead, she lifted up a heavy wooden crate and set it on a shelf, slamming it into place as as subtle hint.

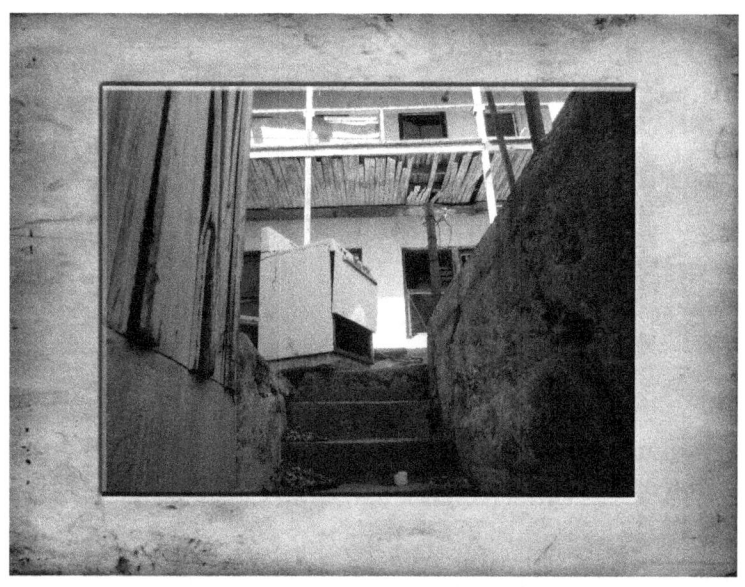

The pair continued to talk without interruption and now she was on the receiving end of more information than she wanted. She already knew more about the habits of the revolving door tenants than she wished to know. Others might enjoy the practice of gossip, but Rosalita did not like knowing too much about people or then she would find it hard to ever rid her mind of the images.

"She isn't going to put up with it this time, I'm sure." One man announced.

Abandoned Places: Abandoned Memories (Desert Edition)

"She can suck my dick! I'm making almost twice as much up here than I did down there. She just won't leave her family. Most people don't even know I'm married. They think I made up the wife."

"Probably doesn't help you had Shelley over last weekend." The other man chuckled.

The first man snorted. "See? I have to find it where I can get it since she's not giving me any."

The men walked away.

Rosalita shook her head. She was certainly used to the colorful language and the men that came and went, but she would never be accustomed to the way men felt they deserved it all, even if they hadn't earned it.

Her late husband came to mind. He drank himself to death, turned yellow and died a most horrible death. He blamed everyone for everything that happened to him in his life and never took responsibility. Her dislike of men in general left a sour taste in her mouth. She was just glad she was older and no longer a woman raising babies and having to depend on a man for money, in managing a family or even in bed. She was thankful that part of her life was over.

Abandoned Places: Abandoned Memories (Desert Edition)

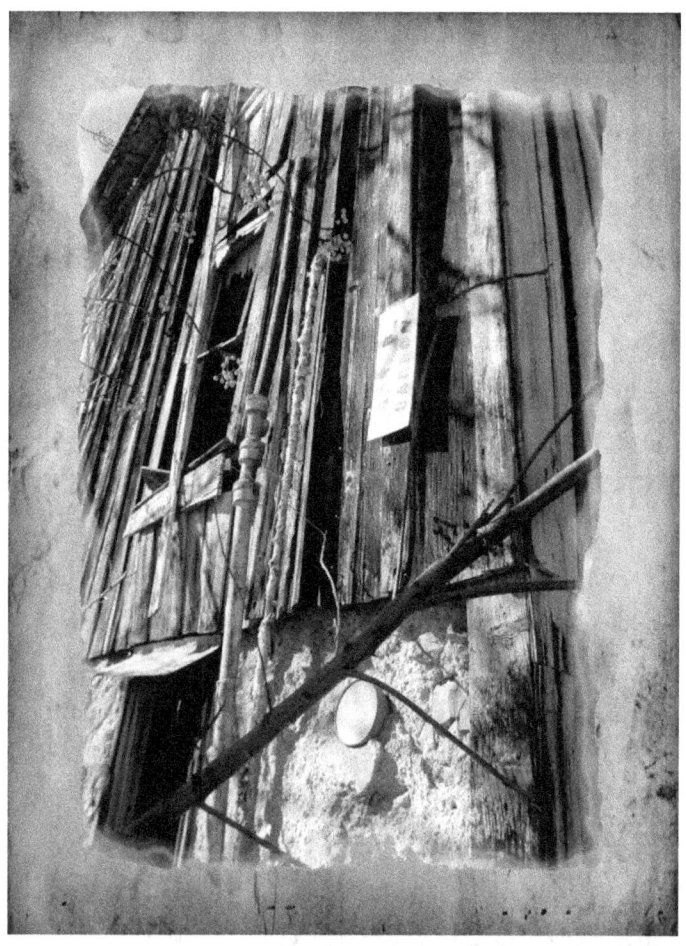

Rosalita left the cool dark room and out into the piercing sunlight. She made her way down to the narrow hillside road and followed the path that was so well known to her that she

Abandoned Places: Abandoned Memories (Desert Edition)

no longer looked around. There was no one she wanted to wave and say "hello." In fact, she doubted anyone even knew she existed. She did a good job of remaining quiet, unassuming and nonthreatening.

The routine had left her mind open to wander, but there was no focus for her day other than the duties to be done and the time on her watch.

She finished the flight of stairs in the hillside and came down onto the street just as a police car rolled by. Rosalita's belly clenched and her instincts told her to step back into the shadows of the stairwell, but then that would cause notice. She willed herself to continue walking robotically in the direction she needed to take, being extra careful to cross the street properly as the police car finished down the street without slowing.

She let out a breath and remembered 30 years ago when she was pregnant and a police car stopped and they climbed out and questioned her. She pretended to not understand the language and then acted as though the baby was coming. The officers took her to the clinic, dropped her off and then got a call and left.

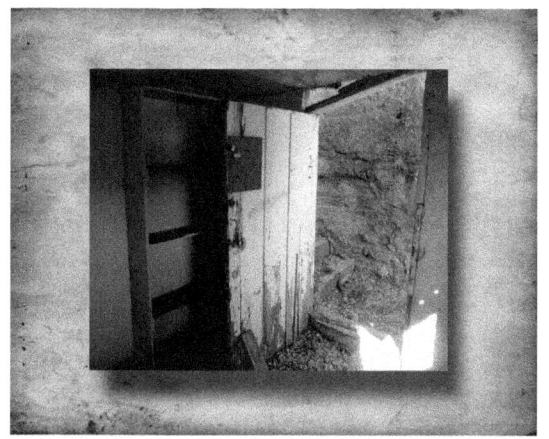

It was her one and only encounter with them and she had learned since then to appear to have a place to go and things to do. They didn't like loitering and they didn't like when people ducked back into buildings when they saw them.

Rosalita stepped into the shop and passed quietly down the aisles to get what she came for. She efficiently purchased what she needed and exited back out into the welcome sunlight.

Someone called out and she tried not to turn and look. She knew they couldn't be calling after her. Then, she heard it again. Her palms began to sweat and she grabbed her bag up tightly to her chest and hurried across the narrow street.

"Ma'am!"

Rosalita took a breath, carefully pivoted to find the woman from the shop rushing up to her,

her tanned face flushed.

"You forgot your other bag." The woman smiled.

Rosalita took it and nodded tightly, turning back to her flight of stairs to the upper roadway. Her heart still skipped anxiously as she rested at the top of the stairs and looked down at the quiet town.

It was strange how that simple set of stairs to her represented entering the dangerous place and getting onto the upper roadway where the vagrant workers and migrant people came and went gave her a safe haven of anonymity amongst the other nameless faces.

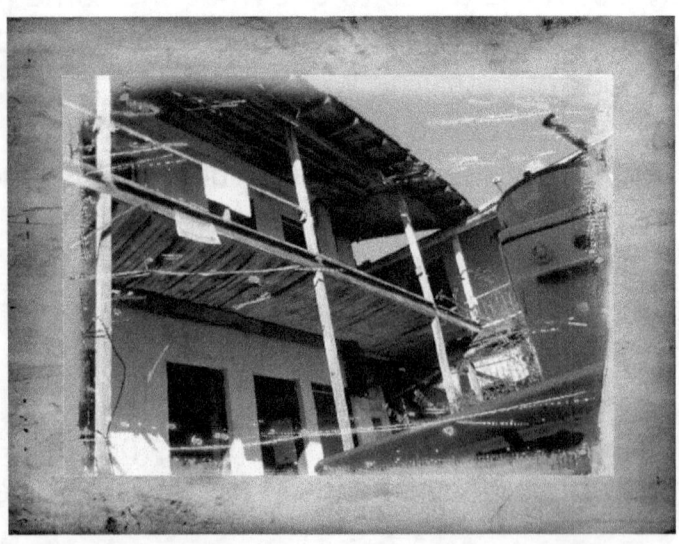

Abandoned Places: Abandoned Memories (Desert Edition)

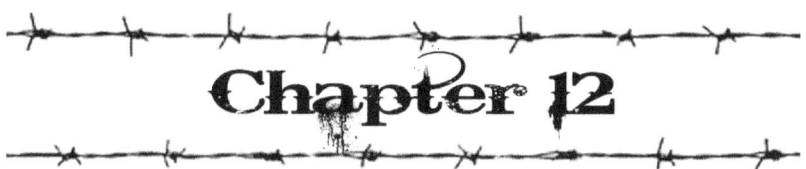

Chapter 12

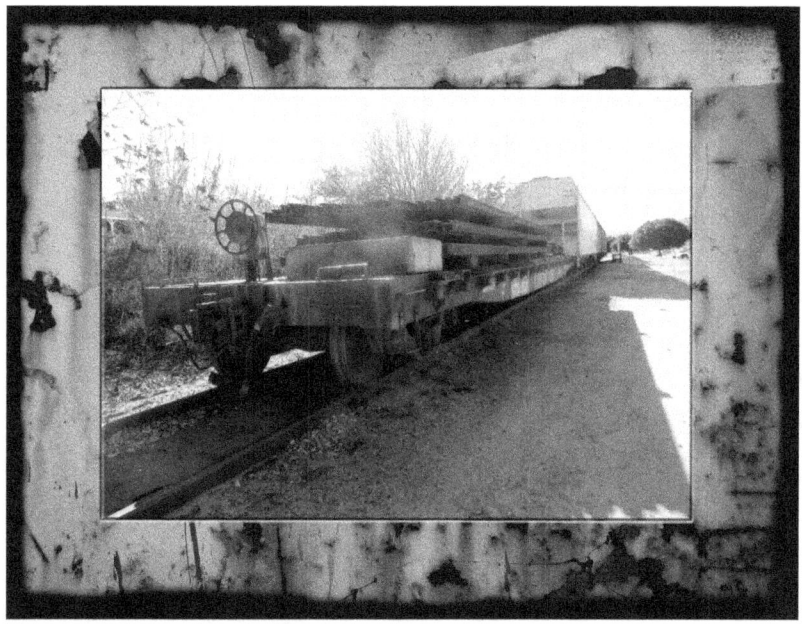

"Harried Engineer"

Abandoned Places: Abandoned Memories (Desert Edition)

We were just wandering around, driving up and down side roads. We kept passing this train sitting on a track and didn't think much of the permanently parked craft. Then, Sharon decided to pull up and check it out. It was, after all, metal and that usually promised clearer reads. A small paper slip on it had it marked as derailing at 22 mph without a known reason.

As we walked up and down the train cars and studied them, it intrigued us to see it up close since it was not something one usually did. Sharon kept her hands at her sides. She didn't want to be distracted by reading all kinds of residual of every curious local who had touched it. There would be so many stories associated with it that it would be hard to find one that she could link with.

Julie inspected it from all angles, clicking off pictures and shaking her head. It was huge and impressive, but there was no doubt Sharon would have a hard time finding just one spot on all that metal to take a read. To her surprise, Sharon came to rest midway along the train.

Thinking about the train and its design, Sharon studied a side ladder handle, the obvious grabbing place to hoist oneself up. Finally, she dared to touch a surface, her fingers slipped around the rung. This time, she received a visual of the man who had touched this surface and then his personality crept in, as did the people he worked with. A dynamic emerged that was too interesting to pass up.

The man came to her mind quite clearly, in his late 30s/early 40s, lean and hard, shorter in stature, sun-worn and a technical career, some sort of mechanical engineer. She wasn't certain he was associated with the train, but he had gripped that handle and left his essence remarkably clearly. What conditions it took to leave an imprint of memory on an object was something Sharon had searched for an answer to. Some items, people could wear like jewelry and not have a memory on it after months. Other times, they could just grab it up and leave a tracer very quickly.

In regards to the metal rung, it was this man's very attitude he approached the world with that caught Sharon's attention. Some people would call it "short man's syndrome," but this posture was defensive all the time, pessimistic and know-it-all. Sharon didn't particularly like the man, but she understood him. Even reading nasty people, a bit of vulnerability showed itself. In this man's case, he was focused on what was wrong with everything. She felt a bit of pity for him for being so clueless.

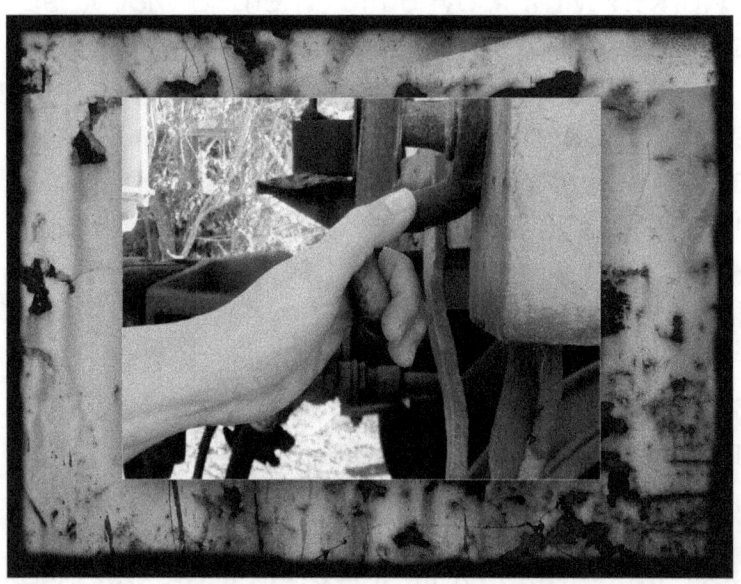

Abandoned Train

"If one more fucking person tells me to calm down, I'm going to punch the closest person."

"Step back." One of the big burly men laughed and held up his arms, backing up just a bit. "Junior is going to spit and hiss."

Abandoned Places: Abandoned Memories (Desert Edition)

The engineer's fists clenched. He wasn't sure if this new crew was mocking his size or his younger years. He wasn't even that young, but compared to these grizzled men, he probably did look like a pup.

No techniques seemed to work with the men. They were hesitant to report issues and tried to rig things themselves and later the engineer would find it and ask who made the brilliant decision. They didn't understand safety or compliance and they really resented having him come in there and remain for longer than expected to see where their weak spots were.

The short and lean engineer hoisted himself up and turned away from the crowd of big-bellied tall men.

He felt more like a terrier nipping at their 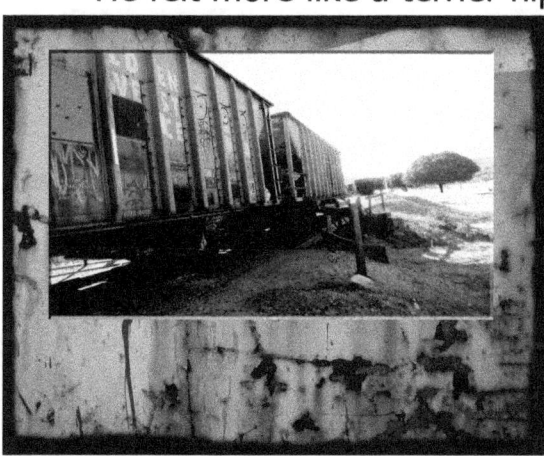 heels. They hardly took his anger seriously. He had tried being nice, being chummy, being cold

Abandoned Places: Abandoned Memories (Desert Edition)

and professional and now being one of the men. Nothing seemed to work to get them to open up.

It didn't help that he always had to look up at them to dictate his orders. His height always bothered him, but never so much as with this crowd. He was supposed to be their superior. It hardly felt like that.

He paced back and forth outdoors and took in a few breaths and then went to his lunch box. One place they all equalized was bringing in their lunches. The engineer sat down on a toolbox and flipped it open, trying not to look back at the men. He knew they were dispersing back to their work, but he also knew that if he looked up at them, his eye contact would engage them in coming over and bothering him some more. They had already enjoyed ridiculing him by putting out the step ladder as if a jab at his height.

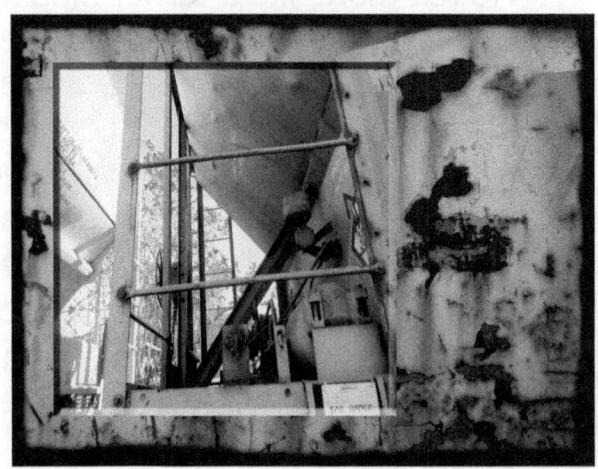

Abandoned Places: Abandoned Memories (Desert Edition)

Not even considering what was happening in his personal life with his separation, the issues with lawyers, the recent illness in his youngest son and his mother getting Alzheimer's, this work seemed like just another example of why his life sucked. It was always someone else's issues that brought him down. He worked hard to not create his own issues, but those around him seemed hell bent on bringing drama to his feet every morning he woke up.

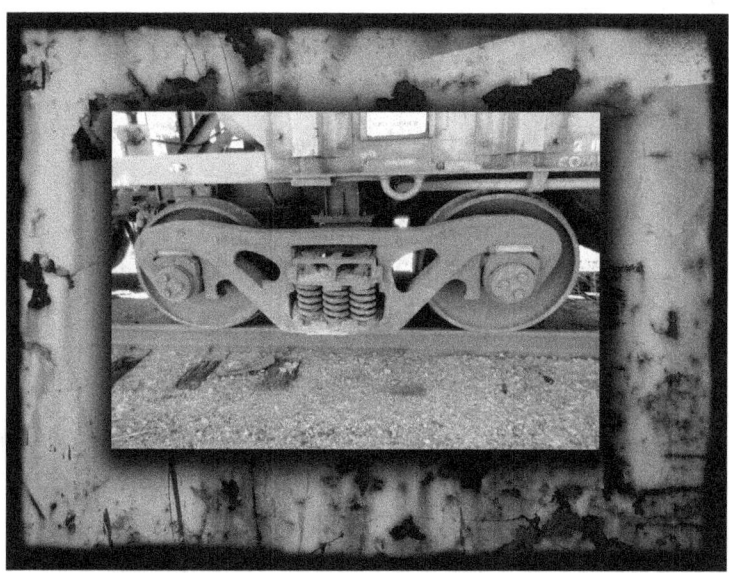

"You know, if you quit approaching everything looking for what's wrong with it, you

Abandoned Places: Abandoned Memories (Desert Edition)

might get a better response. You're making this harder on you than you need to."

The engineer didn't need to turn to know it was the token woman on the team. She remained silent all the time and now that he finally heard her voice, he was surprised at how soft it was considering how hard she appeared.

"What the fuck does that mean?" He chewed a bite off a hunk of cheese, but refused to look up at her as she cast a shadow over his unpleasant picnic.

"You arrive on site and you start ripping into Tommy for his tools. Then, you ask where everyone is, are they yanking off in the yard? Then, you begin to inspect every detail, bitching and moaning the entire time. I fucking feel sorry for your wife, dude." She smarted off.

His head snapped back and he tossed the cheese into the pail.

"Do you come home and start tearing apart everything? You ever try telling someone what's right first before you begin to tell them what's wrong? The only time anyone hears from you is when you're pissed off."

"That's my job, to find things that do no

comply with standards."

"It's not your job to wonder where the work crew is. You're not a supervisor. If Tommy spreads his tools out in an order that works for him, don't ask him to put away every tool when he needs them handy. You think you're all efficient but you're not. You make things harder for yourself by fighting it."

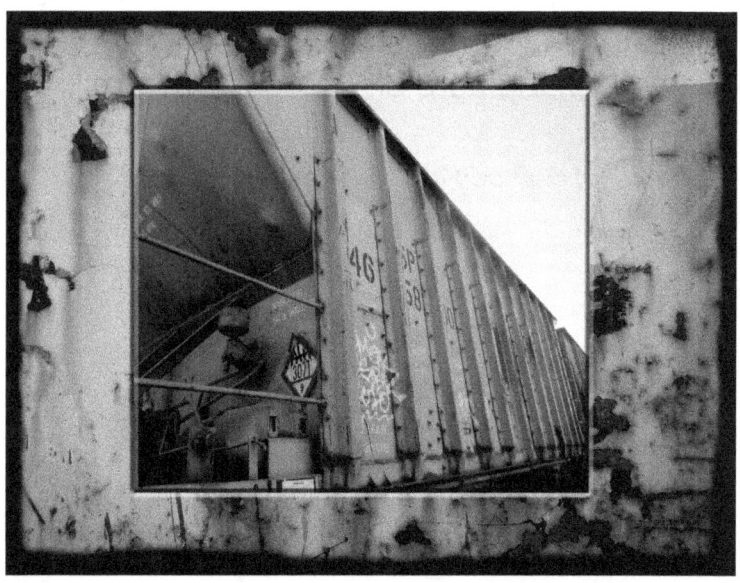

He frowned up at her weather crinkled face.

"I'm just saying." She shrugged and walked off.

Abandoned Places: Abandoned Memories (Desert Edition)

The sunlight blinded him again with her large presence gone. The engineer pushed aside his pail and got up, dusting himself off. The lunch sat like had given him the last time they argued before she told him to leave. What was a stone in his belly.

He was not pleased to hear nearly the same lecture his wife wrong with everyone? He was diligent, hard working and brutally honest. They were just a bunch of babies pouting because he made note of where they were screwing up.

They were obviously insecure, every last one of them!

End